# THE
# YOGHURT
# COOKBOOK

# THE YOGHURT COOKBOOK

*Pamela Westland*

## ELM TREE BOOKS
### LONDON

First published in Great Britain 1979
by Elm Tree Books/Hamish Hamilton Ltd
Garden House, 57–59 Long Acre, London WC2E 9JZ

Copyright © 1979 by Pamela Westland

Illustrations by Dick Barnard

British Library Cataloguing in Publication Data

Westland, Pamela
  The yoghurt cookbook.
  1. Cookery (Yogurt)
  I. Title
  641.6'7'146      TX759
   ISBN 0-241-89763-7

Printed in Great Britain by
Lowe & Brydone Printers Ltd, Thetford, Norfolk

# Contents

# Introduction

At a dinner party a little while ago we were playing the 'desert island' game, asking each other which five basic foods we would take if we were to spend the rest of our lives in stranded isolation. 'Yoghurt,' I said without hesitation. And then had difficulty in thinking of any others I would need. For, to me, yoghurt is the most versatile of foods. It gives lightness in baking, smoothness in sauces and blandness where strong flavours are being used. Its texture, somewhere between liquid and solid, contrasts well with everything from clear soups to crunchy crumbles, and its flavour, somewhere between sweet and sour, offsets both richness and sweetness in other ingredients. Indeed, a spoonful of yoghurt can come to the rescue of many a dish that might otherwise be a near disaster.

Yes, I'd go right back to basics and take yoghurt, hoping that the desert island had some animals – sheep, cows, goats, asses or camels – to provide milk to keep up a continuous supply.

As with so many means of cooking and preserving food, yoghurt is thought to have been discovered by accident, by the nomadic tribesmen crossing the vast Asian continent – or more probably by several groups of people at roughly the same time. The travellers carried fresh milk from one camp to another in bags made from the linings of sheeps' stomachs. The milk, exposed to long days of hot sun in containers not favoured by sterilization processes of any kind, was gradually solidified by the friendly activities of the still-present bacteria. And so yoghurt, the world's first convenience food, was born.

As the nomads settled throughout Asia, the Near and Middle East and Eastern Europe, so the knowledge of how to make and use yoghurt, that miraculous way of preserving milk, travelled with them. For although they are unlikely to have understood the process, they had certainly discovered that it took but a little of one batch of yoghurt, together with more fresh milk, to nurture another.

Yoghurt had a place in the cultures of all the ancient peoples. We know that Abraham thought sufficiently highly of it to serve it to the three men who brought him the glad tidings of the birth of his son, Isaac, and that Pliny referred to it as 'an instrument of pleasure'. But it was not until the sixteenth century that yoghurt was first brought to Western Europe and the eighteenth century that some Turkish immigrants took it to America.

Throughout the centuries yoghurt has been credited with miraculous healing powers. Applied as an external poultice, it is said to have cured insomnia and unsightly complexions alike, and taken medicinally to have cured ulcers, food poisoning and the after-effects of excessive drinking. But perhaps it is best known in its accredited role as 'the milk of eternal life', said to be able to prolong both virility and life.

Leaving aside any medical claims – for this is not a medical book – we have been remarkably slow to appreciate what other nations have known for centuries—that yoghurt, low in both fat and calories, is a convenient, nutritious and simply delicious food.

Some people do not like the taste of it – including, I know, many who have never tasted it. And so I can imagine their reaction to a cookery book in which every recipe features yoghurt as a main ingredient, or as a sauce or dressing to provide interesting blends of flavour and texture. They need not worry. To reassure anyone who has not yet joined the yoghurt fan club, I can tell you that while I was testing the recipes for the book I entertained four friends to a traditional, old-fashioned country weekend. From Friday to Sunday they kindly murmured their appreciation of no less than twelve of these recipes. It was only on Sunday evening, when I confessed, that one of them, feeling cheated, said, 'Oh, but I don't even like the stuff.' They had cheerfully eaten their way through banana nog, prune cheeses, mustard eggs, kipper rarebit, prawn and cheese mousse, cheese pie, raspberry soup, aubergine pasta pie, tandoori fish, honey ice cream, chestnut chocolate cream and date and walnut teabread without once suspecting that every dish had a common, secret ingredient!

Many of the recipes are drawn from my own scrapbook of long-term favourites, but now adapted to use yoghurt in place of cream wherever possible and yoghurt cheese in place of cottage cheese or cream cheese. Those of us who are constantly trying not to put on weight might take comfort from the fact that, with yoghurt, so many dishes – ice cream, for example – can be made with fewer calories, a greatly reduced cholesterol value, and no loss of flavour.

All the recipes can be followed using bought yoghurt, but I imagine that anyone interested enough to buy a book of this kind will soon want to experiment with making yoghurt at home. And so the first chapter is devoted to just that, making yoghurt with all types of milk and with equipment starting at the most basic – a saucepan and a spoon – and working up, if you wish, to an electrical appliance. I guarantee that once you discover how incredibly easy – and cheap – it is, making yoghurt will be built into your daily kitchen routine.

After that, the chapters are planned to take you, healthy and happy, through the day – with yoghurt. I can think of few more pleasant ways to start a day than with a glass of one of the delightfully cool, refreshing yoghurt and fruit drinks, followed by a lovely nutty, crunchy muesli and, if it is Sunday and I am not working, a dish of bacon charlotte or fish cakes.

A whole chapter is given over to those in-between meals, not just breakfast, but not a full-scale lunch. The suggestions are either quick and easy to prepare or can be made the night before and will wait good-temperedly for family and friends to grace the table.

Yoghurt is a natural for all the tea-time treats in Chapter 4, ranging from the spiced, syrupy cakes from Turkey and the rich, tangy cheesecakes of Eastern Europe to our own regional favourites, scones, muffins and teabreads.

The last three chapters present ideas for a dinner party – though they are not, clearly, to be used at random and without discrimination, one creamy, yoghurty sauce following another! There is a section labelled 'off to a good start', full of ideas for soups, fruit and vegetable dishes to give guests the early impression that they are in the hands of a thoughtful hostess, and make them glad they came.

The largest chapter of all, devoted to the most important dish of the day, concerns main courses, all the fish, meat and poultry dishes that are made so much more succulent and tempting with their marinade, sauce or topping of yoghurt. Here, too, are ideas for accompanying vegetable dishes, salads and dressings.

Finally, a whole chapter of puddings, delicious endings to a meal and sure-fire guaranteed to send family and guests away with the lasting, lingering thought that all's well with their world. Many of these recipes use bought fruit-flavoured yoghurt as an integral ingredient or a sauce – a winning way to please the children in the household.

Several years ago, I made my own discovery of yoghurt through the health food shops. I grew to like it, learned to make it, and enjoyed cooking with it. Now one whole book and over two hundred recipes later, I am still devoted. Six little tubs of yoghurt are warm and cosy in my kitchen at this very moment and I anticipate eating them with every bit as much pleasure as I ever did. There's fidelity for you!

PAMELA WESTLAND
Wethersfield, Essex
1978

CHAPTER ONE

# *Making Your Own*

Yoghurt is a living thing, and making it at home has become part of the daily kitchen routine for a great many people. Enthusiastic yoghurt-makers may be heard discussing the ingredients and methods they use with every bit as much earnestness as master chefs or pastrycooks exchanging classic recipes. For although there is only one basic way to make yoghurt – by heating milk and stirring it into a little yoghurt culture or 'starter' from a previous batch – the fact that one can use literally any kind of milk, and attain the necessary constant temperature for its growth in a variety of ways, can make every batch a mini adventure. Because yoghurt is a living thing, one might use identical ingredients to make it day after day, and yet no two consecutive batches need have exactly the same properties. Some batches might be slightly sweeter or more sour than others, some have a greater tendency to separate when a spoon is put in and some, just very, very occasionally, do not 'work' at all.

Yoghurt-making can give satisfaction to all kinds of people, whether they enjoy taking part in a centuries-old tradition and like to get as close as possible to the basic realities of nature, or whether they go swinging along with the mechanized age. I have watched yoghurt being made in the Middle East at sunrise with milk fresh from a goat, and enjoyed it, warm and sprinkled with olive oil and herbs, at sundown. I have watched a friend in an all-electric kitchen casually flip a spoonful of yoghurt into a container of milk, switch on and forget about it. And I have seen yoghurt production in a factory, where the conditions are so completely controlled that every batch can be guaranteed to be of identical characteristics and quality. And in all three cases, the yoghurt was delicious.

1

Making yoghurt at home can perhaps be likened to making ginger beer, each batch brewed from a part of the previous plant. To make your first batch of yoghurt you will need a spoonful of a commercially-prepared natural yoghurt, some from a batch a friend has recently made, or a packet of the powdered culture, which you can buy in a sachet form from health food shops. All you have to do is to mix one teaspoonful of natural yoghurt (never try to start a batch with a flavoured variety) or one measure of the powdered culture with 600 ml (1 pint) of milk and leave it in a warm place for about eight hours to set. It is important to use fresh yoghurt at room temperature; four- or five-day-old yoghurt tends to make the new batch rather sour and acidy. And so, to keep a ready supply of delicious yoghurt, it is better to make it in small quantities every day or every other day, rather than in larger batches at less frequent intervals.

Yoghurt consists of two types of bacteria, *Lactobacillus Bulgaricus* which grows most prolifically at temperatures between 45°C and 47°C (113°F and 116°F), and *Streptococcus Thermophilus*, which grows best between 37°C and 42°C (98°F and 108°F). And so, to provide the ideal nursery for the bacteria, in which they will both multiply most readily, it is advisable to heat the milk before adding it to the yoghurt starter, and to keep it warm for eight hours' setting time. The exact temperature is not critical, but the bacteria will not grow below 32°C (90°F) and are killed when the temperature reaches 48°C (118°F).

It is recommended that all kinds of milk except sterilized milk be brought just to boiling point, simmered for a minute or two, then allowed to cool to just above blood heat, around 43°C (110°F), before being mixed with the yoghurt. Use a thermometer, if you have one, to give you confidence for the first few times; but without one, it is easy to tell when the milk has cooled sufficiently. Stick your finger in it and count to ten, slowly. By that time your finger should be slightly tingling and you will be glad the time is up! One electric yoghurt maker (Salton) provides a specially calibrated thermometer.

It is a matter of personal preference whether you make yoghurt in a number of small, one-portion-sized containers or in a single vessel. I prefer to make it in several small earthenware bowls and use one at a time, as I need it. This way each portion looks as fresh as untrodden snow. When it is made in one large container, there is a chance that the yoghurt will separate slightly into curds and whey when a spoon is put in.

To make yoghurt in small containers, bring the milk to the boil, simmer it, remove any skin that has formed and, reserving two tablespoons of the milk, pour the rest into heatproof containers – cups, bowls, heatproof glasses or strong plastic tubs. Allow the milk to cool to the correct temperature. Mix the reserved milk thoroughly with the yoghurt starter. Then carefully divide the yoghurt starter between the containers, pouring it on top as gently as one pours cream on to Irish coffee. Do not stir it in, but leave it to settle on top. Cover the containers with lids or circles cut from a sheet of polythene and leave them undisturbed for eight hours in a temperature of about 18°C (65°F). How you do this will depend on the kind of appliances you have; you can put the containers on a tray in the warming drawer of an oven or in the airing cupboard; in a roasting pan of warm water over the pilot light of a gas cooker, in an insulated 'hay box' cooker, or in a tin specially padded for the purpose. Some people go to the trouble of lining a large biscuit tin with layers of wadding and covering it with cheerful material such as bright checked cotton gingham.

To make yoghurt in a single large container, simmer and cool the milk as usual. Put the yoghurt starter into the container and very gradually pour on the first two tablespoons of the milk. Mix it thoroughly with the yoghurt, then stir while you pour on the rest. Cover the container and leave it, as described above, in a warm place for eight hours. Most of us already have the ideal container for making yoghurt in this way – a wide-necked vacuum flask. It is absolutely perfect for the job, keeping the milk at a warm, constant temperature while the bacteria get to work.

If airing cupboards and hay boxes seem something of a backward glance in this mechanized age, you can buy electric yoghurt-makers at low cost to control the temperature and provide ideal growing conditions, almost guaranteeing perfect results every time. The instructions accompanying the electrical appliances advise that the milk is first boiled then cooled in the usual way, but sometimes, in a lazy and extravagant mood, I mix cold milk with the starter, put it in the container and leave it switched on for up to sixteen hours.

To a certain extent, you can regulate the flavour of your yoghurt by the length of time you leave it at the incubating temperature. If you like a mild-flavoured yoghurt, you can go some way towards achieving it by removing the yoghurt from the warmth as soon as it starts to thicken. Put it in the refrigerator or a cold place to chill. It will continue to thicken, even at this lower temperature, and will taste slightly sweeter than usual. To give the yoghurt a more acid flavour, increase the incubation time – though not by too much, or the yoghurt will begin to separate and the flavour is likely to become unpleasant, one of the most frequent causes of complaint among beginner makers.

If, once in a while, your yoghurt does not set at all, it is most likely to mean that the milk was either too hot or too cold when it was poured on to the starter, or that the incubating temperature was too low to encourage growth of the bacteria. Another cause of failure could be a trace of detergent or soap powder remaining in the container. As with all forms of food preparation, of course, scrupulous cleanliness is essential.

You will probably notice that your yoghurt will mature as each batch succeeds another. If you start from a commercially-prepared yoghurt, or from a powdered (Bulgarian-type) culture, your first one or two batches are likely to have a very slightly bitter taste. The yoghurt will then progressively sweeten, almost imperceptibly, until one day – perhaps after about ten or twelve batches – you will be aware that a slight sourness has crept in again. This is the time to call it a day. Do not continue to use your own yoghurt as a starter, but buy some more.

There is no such thing as the best kind of milk to use; it is a matter of what is available, or of personal preference. The flavour and, of course, the fat content of the yoghurt will vary according to the milk and you can experiment with different types or combinations to find the recipe you like best.

I usually use the gold-topped 'Channel Island' milk which is delivered to my door; with its thick layer of cream in the bottle, it produces a thick, creamy layer on top of the yoghurt. When supplies of bottled milk are low I use one of the cartons of long-life milk which I always keep in the refrigerator. This produces a blander flavour which is neither better nor worse, just different.

You can use canned evaporated milk, made up to 600 ml (1 pint) with water. Obviously, the greater the proportion of evaporated milk to water, the richer the yoghurt will taste. This milk gives a decidedly caramel flavour and makes a good yoghurt to serve plain as a dessert.

To use powdered milk, mix it as directed on the packet, then make it up to the quantity either with boiled and cooled water or with a mixture of milk and water.

If you use sterilized milk there is a slight saving of time, because you do not have to boil it, but simply bring it up to just above blood heat.

Experiment with combinations of skimmed and homogenized milk, powdered and evaporated milk, milk and cream. Each one will give you a new and different flavour.

For special occasions, try making yoghurt with single cream. It gives very much a *crème brûlée* flavour, and is absolutely sensational served with the first soft fruits of the season.

On the subject of the type of milk to use, I was recently chatting to a Greek goatherd, bemoaning the fact that Greek yoghurt, usually made with fresh goats' milk, is always so much more delicious than my own. 'Well,' he said with a wicked glint, 'you've got a garden, haven't you? Then all you need to do is to keep one goat. They don't eat much. Just all your fruit, vegetables, leaves and flowers. And they don't take much looking after. Just milking at four o'clock every morning. But, as you say, the yoghurt is a good deal more pleasant. I should think it over.' And with that, he went whistling off to his breakfast of warm yoghurt and local honey, which a lifetime of caring for a herd of eight hundred goats had surely earned him. I took his point.


*Stabilizing Yoghurt*

Sometimes you will find that home-made yoghurt has a tendency to separate or curdle when it is cooked in a sauce with meat, poultry or fish. The sauce can be rescued by slow and careful stirring, but the problem can be obviated by stabilizing the yoghurt before use. Many Middle-Eastern recipe books, you will notice, call for stabilized yoghurt in the ingredients list. I tested all these recipes with fresh, unstabilized yoghurt and had no problem, but it is well worth knowing the simple procedure. If your sauce does start to curdle, bring it back to

4

smoothness again by stirring in *beurre-manié*, a walnut of butter with flour worked into it.

To stabilize yoghurt, you will need *either* one egg white or one tablespoon of cornflour for every 1.25 litres (2 pints) of natural yoghurt. Put the yoghurt in a pan over a low heat and stir it until it becomes runny. If you are using an egg white, beat it lightly first, then add it to the yoghurt. If you are using cornflour, mix it with a little cold water or milk to a very smooth, thin paste, then stir it into the yoghurt. Add a pinch of salt and bring the yoghurt and stabilizer slowly to the boil, stirring all the time. It is important to stir slowly, rhythmically and in one direction only – rather a soothing operation, in fact. The aim is not to swish the yoghurt about, but to keep it gently revolving in the pan. When the yoghurt just reaches boiling point, turn the heat down to the lowest setting, stand the pan on an asbestos mat if you have one and leave the yoghurt, uncovered, to simmer for about 10 minutes, when it should be the consistency of thick cream. Never put a lid on the pan during this process, because any drops of condensation falling on to the yoghurt would spoil it. After 10 minutes, remove the pan from the heat and allow the yoghurt to cool, then store it in a covered container in the refrigerator for up to two weeks. Use the stabilized yoghurt in sauces and casseroles as you need it.

*Yoghurt Cheese*
One of the marvellous things about having a ready supply of yoghurt is that you can quickly, easily and cheaply make yoghurt cheese – the curds that remain when the whey is strained off. You can use yoghurt cheese in place of cottage cheese or commercially-prepared soft cream cheese in all kinds of recipes varying from salads and pâtés to cakes and puddings. There is a good commercial cheese-maker (Salton) on the market, but you can also make your own using the following method.

Line a colander with a couple of layers of damp muslin and stand the colander in a large mixing bowl. Pour the yoghurt into the muslin, cover it with another piece of muslin and leave it to drain overnight. Or, in the spirit of the Balkan countries, you can tie the yoghurt in a muslin bag and suspend it over a bowl to catch the drips of whey. These cheese bags are a familiar sight in Greece, hanging outside the kitchen window, while a batch of yoghurt stands on the windowsill catching the warmth of the friendly sun.

Store the yoghurt cheese, or curds, for up to two weeks in a covered container in the refrigerator to serve in sandwiches or to use in the many recipes that follow. Alternatively, you can store your cheese in the traditional Middle-Eastern way, rolled into small walnut-sized balls dropped into a jar of olive oil. The cheese will keep for weeks this way. For a quick snack to serve with drinks, remove some of the cheese balls with a draining spoon, roll them in paprika pepper or chopped walnuts and serve them pierced with cocktail sticks.

Reserve the strained whey and store it in a covered container in the refrigerator for about three or four days. It can be used instead of light stock in soups, sauces, gravy and casserole dishes. In the tea-time chapter, you will also find a way to use it in a fruit cake!

The yield can vary slightly, according to the type of milk and the length of time the yoghurt is left to strain. However, as a general guide, 600 ml (1 pint) of yoghurt will give about 225 g (8 oz) of yoghurt cheese.

CHAPTER TWO

# *Fresh as a Spring Morning*

We all know that breakfast is the most important meal of the day. Every article we ever read on slimming or nutrition tells us so. Yet probably we have all been guilty of deciding to skip it in order to spend another few minutes in bed, gleefully adding the calories thus saved to construct an even bigger meal in the evening.

And of course that is the worst thing we could do. Research shows that we should eat smaller meals at regular intervals: this way, the food is more readily burnt up; less likely therefore to make us put on weight. Add to that the fact that exercise taken straight after a meal is the most beneficial of all, and breakfast has everything going for it. A light, nourishing and, just as important, enjoyable meal first thing in the morning will make the exercise of the day, whether it is shopping, manual work or running up and down stairs at the office, seem less rigorous and tiring.

The British have a centuries-old tradition of gigantic breakfasts, sideboards groaning under the weight of silver dishes of kedgeree and kidneys, ham, steak, chops, bacon, eggs, mushrooms . . . menus that must have needed a very considerable amount of exercise to work off during the day.

These days, with people flying off in all directions to catch the train or school bus or answer the telephone, these early morning indulgences seem something of an anachronism. So perhaps it's time to start building up new traditions for light, healthy breakfasts delicious enough to tempt the most reluctant morning risers.

For many people the first drink of the day, the cup of tea or coffee they enjoy on waking, is the thing that makes them start to tick. This chapter begins,

7

perhaps a little surprisingly, with alternative drinks that look as refreshing as a milk shake on a hot day. These light-as-air concoctions of fruit, honey, eggs and yoghurt, sometimes delicately spiced, can be whipped up in seconds in a blender, or made the night before and kept in the refrigerator or a vacuum flask.

The next 'course' consists of cereals, with a range of the muesli-type mixtures of fruit, bran, oats, nuts, honey, brown sugar and yoghurt we have come to enjoy so much. Mix and mingle the ingredients until you find your own particular favourite, then make up a quantity to store in an airtight container. After the drinks and cereals, there are light dishes, mainly of fruit, that are pretty well irresistible, even to the 'can't touch a thing' brigade.

Those who hanker for a more substantial meal need not despair; they should turn to Chapter 3, which is packed with breakfast dishes worth lingering over until well into lunchtime.


## Apple Spice
A perfect 'eye-opener' in the morning. Delicious, too, to serve as an appetiser for summer lunch in the garden.

*300 ml (10 fl oz) natural yoghurt, chilled*
*150 ml (¼ pint) unsweetened apple juice, chilled*
*1 pinch ground cloves*
*1 tablespoon clear honey*
*1 dessert apple, cored and sliced (or use windfall apples, cubed)*

Put all the ingredients together in a blender and blend for a few seconds at high speed until the mixture is smooth; pour into two glasses and serve.

Without a blender, whisk together the yoghurt, apple juice, clove and honey. Cut the apple into very thin slices. Pour the drink into glasses and float the fruit on top.
*Serves 2*


## Orange Nog
A glass so full of vitamins and protein, it is almost a meal in itself.

*300 ml (10 fl oz) natural yoghurt, chilled*
*½ can frozen unsweetened orange concentrate, thawed*
*1 egg*
*1 tablespoon clear honey*

Whisk or blend the ingredients together until smooth and slightly frothy and pour into glasses.
*Serves 2*

## Grapefruit Cup

*300 ml (10 fl oz) natural yoghurt, chilled*
*1 grapefruit*
*1 egg*
*1 tablespoon clear honey*
*1 dessertspoon fresh mint leaves*
*2 sprigs mint leaves*

Blend together the yoghurt, strained juice of the grapefruit, egg, honey and mint leaves or, without a blender, chop the mint and whisk the ingredients. Pour into two glasses and decorate each with a sprig of mint and a twist of thinly-pared grapefruit skin.
*Serves 2*

## Banana Nog

*300 ml (10 fl oz) natural yoghurt, chilled*
*1 dessertspoon soft light brown sugar*
*1 egg*
*1 banana*
*1 large pinch cinnamon*

Blend the ingredients together, or, without a blender, mash the banana and whisk everything together in a bowl. Pour into two glasses and sprinkle a little extra cinnamon on top of each.
*Serves 2*

## Banana Malt

Malted drinks are not necessarily only for bed-time. They are worth waking up for, too!

*8 rounded teaspoons natural malted milk powder*
*150 ml (¼ pint) hot milk*
*150 ml (5 fl oz) natural yoghurt, chilled*
*1 banana*
*15 g (½ oz) hazelnuts*

Put the malted milk powder into a bowl, slowly pour on the hot milk and mix to a smooth paste. Cool, then put into a blender with the remaining ingredients. Or mash the banana, finely chop the nuts and whisk all the ingredients together. Chill, pour into two glasses and serve each one sprinkled with a little more malted milk powder topped by a hazelnut.
*Serves 2*

### Almond Cream

A very nourishing 'whole food' drink to take the place of a bowl of cereal.

*300 ml (10 fl oz) natural yoghurt, chilled*
*1 tablespoon black treacle*
*1 tablespoon whole almonds*
*1 rounded tablespoon wheat germ*

Put all the ingredients into a blender and blend at high speed for a few seconds until the almonds have 'disappeared'. Or grind the almonds in a food mill and whisk all the ingredients together. Pour into two pottery beakers and sprinkle each with a little extra wheat germ.
*Serves 2*

### Coffee Yoghurt

Early-morning coffee drinkers might like to try this new and nourishing way of taking their favourite brew.

*2 tablespoons strong percolated coffee or 4 teaspoons instant*
*    coffee dissolved in 4 teaspoons hot water*
*300 ml (10 fl oz) natural yoghurt, chilled*
*1 egg*
*1 tablespoon clear honey*
*1 pinch ground nutmeg or mace*

Whisk or blend the ingredients together and pour into two glasses. Serve chilled, sprinkled with a little more spice.
*Serves 2*

### Tomato on the Rocks

An any-time drink, perfect before a meal or at parties, before driving home.

*2 125-ml (¹/₅-pint) bottles tomato juice, chilled*
*150 ml (5 fl oz) natural yoghurt, chilled*
*1 teaspoon fresh mint or basil leaves*
*a few drops Worcestershire sauce or red pepper sauce*
*chipped ice cubes to serve*

Mix the ingredients together in a blender, or chop the herb leaves and then whisk everything together in a bowl. Serve poured over chipped ice cubes.
*Serves 2*

### Chocolate Whip

*2 tablespoons drinking chocolate*
*1 tablespoon hot water*
*300 ml (10 fl oz) natural yoghurt, chilled*

*a few chocolate drops* or *chocolate buttons*
*1 chocolate milk flake*

Mix the chocolate powder to a smooth paste with the hot water, cool, then whisk with the chilled yoghurt. Stir in the chocolate drops or buttons, chill and pour into two glasses. Sprinkle each one with a little crumbled milk flake bar, and serve with a spoon.
*Serves 2*

## Lemon Whip
The addition of whipped egg white makes a light, frothy drink resembling a milk shake.

*150 ml (5 fl oz) natural yoghurt, chilled*
*2 tablespoons clear honey*
*juice of ½ lemon*
*1 egg white, stiffly beaten*
*lemon slices to decorate*

Whisk together the yoghurt, honey and lemon juice, and then, using a metal spoon, fold in the stiffly-beaten egg white. Pour into 2 glasses and decorate each one with a slice of lemon resting on the rim of the glass.
*Serves 2*

## Fruit Whips
You can make flavoured yoghurt drinks with any fresh, dried or frozen fruits of your choice.

*150 ml (5 fl oz) natural yoghurt, chilled*
*300 ml (½ pint) chilled fruit purée made from fresh or frozen*
*    strawberries or raspberries, fresh or dried apricots, prunes, canned*
*    pineapple etc.*
*clear honey to sweeten (optional)*
*1 egg white, stiffly beaten*
*fruit to decorate*

Whisk together the yoghurt and fruit purée. Sweeten if necessary with a little clear honey. Using a metal spoon, fold in the stiffly-beaten egg white and pour into four glasses. Serve at once with a little fresh or preserved fruit, if available, or with a sprig of herb.
*Serves 4*

## Ayran
In Turkey one of the most familiar sights is the yoghurt-drink man, carrying a large bronze bowl and a dozen or so goblets on a yoke over his shoulders. This is a drink for a really hot day when the very lightness of the beverage is refreshing.

*150 ml (5 fl oz) natural yoghurt, chilled*
*150 ml (¹/₄ pint) iced water*
*1 pinch salt*
*1 teaspoon fresh chopped mint leaves*

Whisk the ingredients together and serve ice cold in chilled glasses.
*Serves 2*


## Spiced Porridge

For purists, porridge is served with salt and milk or cream. It's delicious with these ingredients, too.

*600 ml (1 pint) water*
*175 g (6 oz) oats*
*¹/₂ teaspoon salt*
*150 ml (5 fl oz) yoghurt*
*ground cinnamon*
*clear honey* or *soft light brown sugar (optional)*

Bring the water to the boil in a pan, sprinkle on the oats and salt, stir with a wooden spoon, then cover and simmer over a low heat for 30 minutes, stirring occasionally. Add a little more water if necessary. Serve the porridge in shallow bowls. Top each one with a spoonful of yoghurt sprinkled lightly with cinnamon. Sweeten if necessary with clear honey or sugar.
*Serves 4*


## Orange Muesli

The first time I served muesli everyone pronounced it 'dry old stuff'. It took a long time to tempt them to try again – which I did by soaking the oatmeal overnight.

*4 tablespoons medium oatmeal*
*180 ml (just over ¹/₃ pint) water*
*1 orange*
*2 dessert apples, cored and grated*
*50 g (2 oz) candied peel, chopped*
*25 g (1 oz) shelled walnuts, chopped*
*300 ml (10 fl oz) natural yoghurt*
*soft light brown sugar (optional)*

Put the oatmeal in a container, pour on the water, stir well, cover and leave a while to soak. Stir in the grated rind and strained juice of the orange, the grated apple, and the chopped peel and walnuts. Divide into 4 serving bowls. Serve with yoghurt and sweeten, if necessary, with soft brown sugar.
*Serves 4*

### 'Instant' Muesli
Make this mixture in larger quantities and store it in an airtight tin for an instant cereal.

*100 g (4 oz) quick porridge oats*
*25 g (1 oz) sultanas*
*25 g (1 oz) stoneless raisins*
*25 g (1 oz) blanched almonds, chopped*
*milk to mix*
*425-g (15-oz) can guavas, chopped*
*natural yoghurt to serve*

Mix together the oats, sultanas, raisins, and almonds and mix to a creamy consistency with milk. Pour into a serving dish and top with the chopped guavas. Serve the yoghurt – a delightful partner to the fruit – separately.
*Serves 4*


### Date Muesli
This muesli, with condensed milk, is strictly for those with a sweet tooth. Others could substitute 150 ml (5 fl oz) natural yoghurt.

*4 heaped tablespoons oat flakes*
*150 ml (¼ pint) water*
*4 tablespoons condensed milk (or use yoghurt)*
*1 lemon*
*50 g (2 oz) stoned dates, chopped*
*2 dessert apples, cored and grated*
*2 bananas, sliced*
*50 g (2 oz) hazelnuts, chopped*
*300 ml (10 fl oz) natural yoghurt*

Put the oats in a bowl and add the water and condensed milk or 150 ml (5 fl oz) natural yoghurt. Stir well, cover and leave overnight. Next day, add the grated rind of half the lemon, all the strained juice and the dates, grated apple and sliced banana. Divide the muesli between 4 bowls, sprinkle with the chopped nuts and serve with natural yoghurt – which largely combats the sweetness of the dish.
*Serves 4*


### Buckwheat Muesli

*4 tablespoons toasted buckwheat*
*120 ml (⅕ pint) water*
*1 tablespoon wheat germ*
*50 g (2 oz) hazelnuts, chopped*
*100 g (4 oz) seedless grapes*

*2 dessert apples, cored and grated*
*2 tablespoons sultanas*
*juice of ¹/₂ lemon*
*1 tablespoon clear honey*
*300 ml (10 fl oz) natural yoghurt*

Soak the buckwheat overnight in the water, then stir in the remaining ingredients except the yoghurt. Serve the muesli in bowls with the yoghurt handed round separately.
*Serves 4*

## All-seasons Fruit Bowl
One of the worst gastronomic experiences of my schooldays was when I was staying for the holidays with a friend, and discovered we were allowed nothing but stewed prunes for breakfast every day. But a bowl of chilled mixed dried fruits is delightful, and especially convenient for a busy hostess with a house full of guests.

*100 g (4 oz) dried figs, trimmed*
*100 g (4 oz) dried apricots*
*100 g (4 oz) dried prunes*
*100 g (4 oz) dried apple rings*
*600 ml (1 pint) water*
*225 g (8 oz) soft light brown sugar*
*1 lemon*
*1 teaspoon mixed spice*
*600 ml (20 fl oz) natural yoghurt, chilled*
*2 drops cinnamon essence*

Wash the fruits and leave them, mixed, to soak overnight in the water. Next day, strain the water into an enamel saucepan, add the sugar, thinly-pared lemon rind, strained lemon juice and spice and bring to simmering point. Simmer the syrup for 10 minutes, add the strained fruit and simmer for about 45 minutes, until tender. Serve with natural yoghurt stirred with the cinnamon essence.
*Serves 4–6*

## Melon Baskets
Melon is as refreshing as the dew on the grass: elegant for a dinner party, invigorating for breakfast.

*1 yellow-skinned melon*
*1 orange*
*1 grapefruit*
*soft light brown sugar (optional)*
*300 ml (10 fl oz) natural yoghurt*

Cut a very small slice from one 'long' side of the melon so that it stands without rocking. Slice about one-third off the top of the melon, lengthwise, and use scissors or a knife to cut a zig-zag pattern around the rim. Using a grapefruit knife or a tablespoon, scoop out the flesh, discard the seeds and chop the flesh into cubes. Peel the orange and grapefruit and divide them into segments, discarding the skin and pips. Mix the fruit together, and sweeten with brown sugar if necessary. Stir in the yoghurt, pile the fruit into the melon shell, stand on a serving plate and chill.
*Serves 4–6*

## Stuffed Prune Cheeses
The black and white contrast of this dish is one of its advantages; the blend of sweet and sharp flavours another.

*450 g (1 lb) prunes*
*300 ml (½ pint) dry cider*
*225 g (8 oz) yoghurt cheese (see page 5)*
*salt*
*grated nutmeg*
*600 ml (20 fl oz) natural yoghurt*

Soak the prunes in the cider overnight. Next day, bring to boiling point and simmer for 15 minutes, then strain. Remove the stones and then, using a piping bag, stuff the prunes with the yoghurt cheese lightly seasoned with salt. Stir a little grated nutmeg into the yoghurt and pour it into a flat serving dish. Carefully lay the prunes on top, sprinkle with a little more spice and serve chilled.
*Serves 4*

## Orange and Grapefruit Grill
The interest in this dish is the surprise contrast of the grilled fruit and chilled yoghurt. Bring it to the table the second it is ready, or the drama is lost!

*2 grapefruit*
*2 oranges*
*100 g (4 oz) soft dark brown sugar*
*300 ml (10 fl oz) natural yoghurt, chilled*

Skin the grapefruit and oranges, divide them into segments and discard the skin and pips. Spread the fruit evenly in the bottom of a shallow, heatproof dish and cover completely with the sugar. Put under a hot grill for 3–4 minutes until the sugar caramellizes. Quickly spread the yoghurt over, and serve at once.
*Serves 4*

## Toasted Buckwheat Bake
Buckwheat is the staple cereal of Russia, taking the place there of our porridge oats and cornflakes. This creamy egg dish makes a light yet filling meal.

*175 g (6 oz) toasted buckwheat*
*450 ml (³/₄ pint) milk*
*150 ml (5 fl oz) natural yoghurt*
*100 g (4 oz) yoghurt cheese (see page 5)*
*2 eggs, beaten*
*salt*
*clear honey and natural yoghurt to serve*

Mix together the toasted buckwheat, milk, yoghurt, yoghurt cheese and beaten eggs and season lightly with salt. Pour the mixture into a greased shallow baking dish and bake at 180°C(350°F)/Gas 4, for 35–40 minutes, until the top is golden brown. Serve with honey and natural yoghurt.
*Serves 4*

## Waffles
Much as I love waffles, I find I am often put off by the syrupy accompaniments, which are usually far too sweet for me. But yoghurt does the trick, by adding a welcome sharpness.

*175 g (6 oz) flour*
*pinch salt*
*3 teaspoons baking powder*
*25 g (1 oz) caster sugar*
*2 eggs, separated*
*300 ml (¹/₂ pint) milk*
*50 g (2 oz) butter, melted*
*175 g (6 oz) clear honey*
*juice of 1 lemon*
*450 ml (15 fl oz) natural yoghurt, whipped*

Sift the flour, salt and baking powder into a bowl and stir in the sugar. Make a well in the centre and drop in the egg yolks. Mix with a wooden spoon, gradually adding the milk and butter alternately. Whisk the egg whites until stiff but not dry and fold them into the batter with a wooden spoon.

Grease a waffle iron with a little melted butter or vegetable oil and heat it. Spoon some batter into the waffle iron, tipping it so that it spreads evenly over the surface. Cook the waffles according to the maker's instructions, until crisp and golden brown.

If you do not have a waffle iron, cook the batter as if you were making drop scones. Grease and heat a heavy frying pan and drop in spoonfuls of the batter. Cook for 2–3 minutes on each side.

Serve the waffles hot. Heat the honey in a small pan. Stir in the lemon juice and pour into a jug. Top each waffle with whipped yoghurt.
*Makes 16–20 waffles*

**CHAPTER THREE**

# *Hungry as a Hunter*

People who do an hour's gardening, clean the car or take the dog for a walk before breakfast, arrive at the kitchen door with all the appearances of someone who has earned a hearty meal. On the other hand, those of us who like occasionally to laze the morning away reading the Sunday papers in bed, might think it best to make breakfast and lunch a combined effort.

Recipes in this chapter should satisfy both needs. They are, in the main, substantial without being stodgy; filling yet not too fiddly to prepare. And in many cases they can be prepared to quite an advanced stage the evening before.

Most families will find dishes here that will become favourites for high-tea and supper, too. On days when everyone seems to be using the house as a snack-bar, it makes sense to prepare quick and easy meals, rather than run the risk of expensive ingredients being spoiled by waiting. Cheese lends itself to these between-time meals. Yoghurt cheese blends naturally with all dairy foods and in these recipes it is teamed often with farmhouse cheese. For everyday dishes, you will probably use the cheese you regularly have in the refrigerator, Cheddar, perhaps, or Gouda. Slightly more special occasions might call for one of the 'holey' cheeses that cook so well, Gruyère or Emmenthal, and best of all, for smooth sauces and crunchy toppings, Parmesan.

So here's to breakfast, brunch, lunch, high-tea and supper – the most versatile recipes in the book!

### Wholemeal Pancakes

Wholemeal pancakes filled with melting yoghurt cheese are as delicious for breakfast as scones and cream for tea.

17

*100 g (4 oz) wholemeal flour*
*pinch salt*
*1 egg*
*300 ml (¹/₂ pint) milk*
*oil for frying (see method)*
*225 g (8 oz) yoghurt cheese (see page 5)*
*1 tablespoon seedless raisins*
*cinnamon*

Sift together the flour and salt into a bowl, add the egg, then gradually beat in the milk to make a smooth batter. You can prepare the batter the night before, and store it in the refrigerator.

Heat 1 tablespoon oil in an omelette pan or heavy-bottomed frying pan and, when the oil is smoking hot, pour in enough batter to cover the base, tipping the pan to spread the batter evenly. Fry for 2–3 minutes until the batter is set, then flip the pancake over and fry the other side until the surface is golden brown. Keep the pancakes hot while you fry the remainder. Add more oil as needed.

Spread each pancake with yoghurt cheese, sprinkle with raisins and roll up. Serve on a hot serving dish, lightly sprinkled with cinnamon.
*Serves 4*

## Bacon Charlotte
A light lunch or supper dish that combines bacon, apples and cheese in a quick and tasty way. It can be prepared the night before, ready to cook in the morning.

*225 g (8 oz) bacon rashers*
*100 g (4 oz) butter*
*225 g (8 oz) fresh white breadcrumbs*
*3 large cooking apples, peeled, cored and grated*
*50 g (2 oz) yoghurt cheese (see page 5)*
*175 g (6 oz) cheese, grated*
*salt*
*freshly-ground black pepper*
*1 teaspoon dried mint*
*¹/₂ teaspoon made mustard*

Grease a shallow, ovenproof dish.

Cut the rind from the bacon rashers. Reserving 4 whole rashers, chop the remaining ones. Melt the butter in a pan and add the bacon, frying just until the fat begins to run. Stir in the breadcrumbs, grated apple, yoghurt cheese and three-quarters of the grated cheese. Season well with salt and pepper and add the dried mint and mustard. Spread the mixture in the ovenproof dish, sprinkle with the remaining grated cheese and criss-cross with the reserved bacon rashers. Bake at 180°C(350°F)/Gas 4 for 45 minutes. Serve hot.
*Serves 4*

## Cheese Eggs

In Britain, we lag behind our European neighbours in the amount of cheese we serve for breakfast. Here it provides a melting foundation for fried eggs.

*100 g (4 oz) Edam Cheese*
*40 g (1½ oz) unsalted butter*
*4 eggs*
*paprika pepper*
*150 ml (5 fl oz) natural yoghurt*
*few sprigs parsley*

Cut the cheese into 4 thick slices. Melt the butter in a frying pan until hot, then fry the cheese slices for 3–4 minutes on each side. Set aside and keep warm while you fry the eggs – add a little more fat to the pan. Place the cheese slices on a hot serving dish, top each one with a fried egg and sprinkle with paprika pepper. Spoon the yoghurt over, sprinkle with another pinch of pepper and serve garnished with parsley. Fingers of toast or rye crispbread go well with this rather rich dish.

## Mushroom Rarebit

This comes to the table looking rather like a rich pâté, but inside it's mushrooms and bread and cheese and eggs.

*4 thick slices white bread, without crusts*
*50 g (2 oz) butter*
*100 g (4 oz) mushrooms, wiped and thinly sliced*
*salt*
*freshly-ground black pepper*
*8 eggs*
*2 tablespoons natural yoghurt*
*1 tablespoon beer*
*100 g (4 oz) cheese, grated*
*½ teaspoon made mustard*

Cut the bread diagonally, into triangles. Heat half the butter in a frying pan and fry the bread until it is crisp and brown on one side. Arrange the shapes, fried side down, in one layer in the base of an ovenproof dish. Cover with a layer of mushrooms and season well with salt and pepper. Break the eggs on top. Melt the rest of the butter, remove from the heat and stir in the yoghurt, beer, cheese and mustard. Spoon this mixture over the eggs, taking care not to break them. Bake at 220°C(425°F)/Gas 7 for 20–25 minutes, until brown and bubbling. Serve with hot, buttered toast.
*Serves 4–6*

## Kipper Rarebit

*1 275-g (10-oz) packet frozen kippers*
*150 g (5 oz) cheese, grated*
*15 g (¹/₂ oz) butter*
*2 tablespoons natural yoghurt*
*2 tablespoons beer*
*1 teaspoon made mustard*
*pinch cayenne pepper*
*salt*
*freshly-ground black pepper*
*4 slices of hot, buttered toast to serve*

Cook the kippers according to the instructions on the packet. Drain them and skin and flake the fish. You can leave the fish, covered, overnight in the refrigerator.

Put the grated cheese, butter, yoghurt, beer, mustard and seasonings into a small pan and heat gently, stirring until the mixture is smooth. Add the flaked fish and continue cooking and stirring for 1–2 minutes to heat the fish. Do not allow the mixture to boil. Pile the mixture on to the hot, buttered toast and grill until bubbling and golden. Serve at once.
*Serves 4*

## Pineapple Grill

Piled high with goodies attractively arranged, this looks rather like a grilled Danish open sandwich.

*4 slices of bread, toasted*
*prepared mustard*
*225 g (8 oz) yoghurt cheese (see page 5)*
*4 pineapple rings*
*1 large dessert apple, peeled and sliced*
*cinnamon*
*40 g (1¹/₂ oz) soft dark brown sugar*

Spread the toast first with a little mustard, then with yoghurt cheese. Place a pineapple ring on each one, arrange the apple slices in a pattern and sprinkle with cinnamon and brown sugar. Place under a hot grill and grill until the sugar becomes crisp.
*Serves 4*

## Surprise Toasts

Not perhaps an everyday breakfast snack, but pretty for a holiday or celebration. You can make the toast boxes the night before, assemble the various ingredients and present an imaginative array.

*1 large, day-old uncut white loaf*
*75 g (3 oz) butter*
*2 teaspoons mustard powder*
*a variety of fillings (see method)*

Make little boxes like vol-au-vent cases, from thick slices of bread, and cook them in a very hot oven. This can be done in advance, and the cases stored in an airtight tin, to be re-heated when needed. The fillings can be hot or cold, or you can prepare some of each.

To make the boxes, pre-heat the oven to 230°C(450°F)/Gas 8. Cut the bread into slices 7.5 cm (3 in) thick and trim off the crusts. Using a 7.5-cm (3-in) pastry cutter, cut circles from the bread slices. Then, with a sharp knife, incise a ring about 1 cm (½ in) from the edge, but do not cut right through. Push this centre ring firmly down to leave a depression for the filling. Melt the butter in a small pan and stir in the mustard powder. With a pastry brush, brush the tops and sides of the boxes. Place them on a lightly-greased baking tray and bake in the hot oven for 6–8 minutes, until they are crisp and light brown. Check after 5 minutes, as at this temperature even a minute or two makes all the difference. If you are serving the boxes straightaway, pile in the filling while the cases are warm. Otherwise, remove them to a wire rack, allow to cool, and store in an airtight tin. To re-heat, place on a baking tray in the oven at 180°C(350°F)/Gas 4 for 15 minutes.

For hot fillings, lightly scramble an egg with a dessertspoon of natural yoghurt and a teaspoon of chives. Top with crumbled fried bacon or a mushroom. Or add finely-chopped cooked chicken or flaked smoked haddock to the scrambled egg mixture. Or mix finely-chopped fried bacon into equal quantities of melted cheddar and yoghurt cheese.

For cold fillings, mix chopped hard-boiled eggs with natural yoghurt, chopped chives and a pinch of cayenne pepper; blend yoghurt cheese with chopped sardines or anchovies, or with an equal quantity of Danish blue cheese.

Decorate each box with a simple garnish – a slice of tomato, cucumber or lemon, sprigs of parsley, chopped herbs or a grinding of pepper.


## Mustard Eggs

There's a pleasant sharpness to this sauce that is quite refreshing. The dish can also be served as an accompaniment to cold, boiled ham.

*40 g (1½ oz) butter*
*40 g (1½ oz) flour*
*300 ml (½ pint) milk, hot*
*150 ml (5 fl oz) natural yoghurt*
*1½ tablespoons Dijon mustard*
*½ tablespoon capers*

*freshly-ground black pepper*
*6 eggs, hard boiled and shelled*
*salt*

Melt the butter in a small pan, sprinkle on the flour and stir until a smooth paste is formed. Gradually pour in the milk and stir until smooth. Cook, stirring, over a moderate heat for 4 minutes, then stir in the yoghurt. Add the mustard and capers and season well with salt and pepper.

Halve the hard-boiled eggs and arrange them, cut side up, in a shallow serving dish. Pour over the sauce and serve with rye bread or pumpernickel.
*Serves 4–6*

### Spiced Sausages
More suitable, I think, for brunch or supper than for an early-morning dish. Remember to start by marinating the sausages for 8–12 hours before cooking.

*450 g (1 lb) chipolata sausages*
*300 ml (10 fl oz) natural yoghurt*
*1 medium-sized onion, skinned and finely chopped*
*grated rind and juice of ¹/₂ lemon*
*salt*
*freshly-ground black pepper*
*¹/₂ teaspoon ground ginger*
*1 teaspoon curry powder*
*1 tablespoon chopped mint*

Put the sausages in a shallow dish with the remaining ingredients, stir well, cover and leave to marinate overnight, or for 8–12 hours. Stir occasionally if it is convenient.

To cook, remove the sausages from the marinade, drain them and cook under a hot grill, turning once, until they are golden brown and cooked through. Heat the marinade in a small pan and serve separately as a sauce. For a more substantial supper dish, serve the sausages accompanied by dishes of mango chutney, toasted nuts, desiccated coconut and fingers of toast.
*Serves 4*

### Danish Pan-fry
Frying pans and omelette pans are so attractive now that they make perfectly acceptable cooker-to-table ware – a great time saver.

*225 g (8 oz) middlecut or streaky bacon rashers*
*1 large onion, skinned and chopped*
*675 g (1¹/₂ lb) potatoes, peeled*
*1 egg, beaten*
*2 tablespoons natural yoghurt*

*freshly-ground black pepper*
*25 g (1 oz) butter*
*1 tablespoon vegetable oil*

For garnish *(optional)*
*25 g (1 oz) butter*
*1 large onion, skinned and cut into rings*

Cut the rind from the bacon rashers and cut them into squares. Put the bacon and onion into a frying pan over moderate heat, stirring at first until the fat begins to melt. Add a little butter if necessary. Fry for 5–6 minutes, until the onion is soft but not brown.

Halve the potatoes and partly cook them in boiling, salted water for 5–10 minutes, depending on the variety. They must not become soft or floury. Drain the potatoes and allow them to cool slightly, then coarsely grate them into a bowl, add the bacon and onion, beaten egg, yoghurt and pepper. Mix well.

Heat the butter and oil in a small omelette pan and turn the potato mixture into it. Spread the mixture evenly over the pan and cook over a moderate heat for about 10–12 minutes, until the under-side is brown, then place the pan under a moderate grill to brown the top lightly.

For the garnish, melt the butter in the original frying pan and fry the onion rings over a moderate heat until they are soft and light brown. Stir them occasionally to prevent burning.
*Serves 4*


## Cheese and Kipper Bake

Any well-flavoured fish, such as smoked haddock or smoked mackerel could be used instead of the kippers; and prawns cooked in this way are delicious.

*450 g (1 lb) potatoes, peeled and thinly sliced*
*450 g (1 lb) yoghurt cheese (see page 5)*
*225 g (8 oz) kipper fillets, skinned and cut into strips*
*1 small onion, skinned and grated or finely chopped*
*1 tablespoon fresh chopped parsley*
*salt*
*freshly-ground black pepper*

For topping
*300 ml (10 fl oz) natural yoghurt*
*2 eggs*
*pinch cayenne pepper*
*1 sprig parsley to garnish*
*1 hard-boiled egg to garnish*

Grease a 1.75-litre (3-pint) pie dish.

Make layers of potato slices, yoghurt cheese and kipper, seasoning each layer with grated onion, chopped parsley, salt and pepper. Begin and end with a potato layer. Place the dish in a roasting tin of warm water and bake at 190°C(375°F)/Gas 5 for 45–50 minutes, or until the potato is cooked.

Beat together the yoghurt, eggs and cayenne pepper, pour over the potatoes and return to the oven for a further 20 minutes. Garnish with the sprig of parsley and sliced hard-boiled egg and serve hot.
*Serves 4–6*


## Fish Cakes

Traditional as a breakfast dish, home-made fish cakes have been somewhat superseded by the commercial varieties. This recipe, using a panada of bread and milk as the thickening agent, gives a lighter texture than the more usual rice or mashed potato.

*225 g (8 oz) cooked fish*
*2 1.5-cm (³/₄-in)-thick slices white bread*
*150 ml (¹/₄ pint) milk, hot*
*2 tablespoons natural yoghurt*
*2 eggs, beaten*
*salt*
*freshly-ground black pepper*
*1 tablespoon chopped parsley*
*pinch dill seed*
*breadcrumbs*
*butter for frying*

Remove all the skin and bones from the fish and mash it well in a bowl. Crumble the bread in another bowl, pour on the hot milk and leave to infuse for 15 minutes. Strain off any excess milk and add the bread to the fish. Stir in the yoghurt and 1 beaten egg, and season with salt, pepper, parsley and dill seed. Divide into eight and shape into rounds. Dip each cake in the remaining beaten egg and roll in breadcrumbs.

Melt the butter in a frying pan. When it is hot, fry the fish cakes for 4–5 minutes on each side until golden brown.
*Serves 4*


## Smoked Haddock Cocottes

You can prepare the cocottes the night before and leave them, ready to cook in the morning. Ideally, leave them in the oven with the timer pre-set for breakfast.

*225 g (8 oz) smoked haddock, cooked, skinned and flaked*
*225 g (8 oz) yoghurt cheese (see page 5)*
*1 medium-sized onion, skinned and chopped*

*100 g (4 oz) mushrooms, wiped and chopped*
*2 eggs, beaten*
*juice of 1 lemon*
*salt*
*freshly-ground black pepper*
*1 tablespoon fresh chopped parsley*

Grease four cocotte or ramekin dishes.

Mix together the flaked fish, yoghurt cheese, onion and mushrooms. Add the eggs to the fish mixture, then the lemon juice, salt, pepper and chopped parsley, reserving a little for garnish. Spoon the mixture into the greased cocotte dishes and stand them in a roasting tin of water. Bake at 180°C(350°F)/Gas 4 for 35–40 minutes, until the mixture is well set. Garnish with the reserved parsley and serve hot with fingers of hot, buttered toast.

*Serves 4*

## Herrings with Watercress Sauce

When brunch can be a leisurely affair, herrings with a zingy stuffing and a light sauce are most enjoyable. Consistently cheaper than those family favourites cod and haddock, they make budget sense for lunch and supper too.

*4 herrings, heads removed, and cleaned*
*1/2 lemon*
*salt*
*freshly-ground black pepper*
*25 g (1 oz) butter*
*1 small onion, skinned and finely chopped*
*100 g (4 oz) button mushrooms, wiped and chopped*
*1/2 bunch watercress, washed, picked over and chopped*

For sauce
*300 ml (10 fl oz) natural yoghurt*
*1/2 bunch watercress, chopped (reserve a few sprigs for garnish)*
*1/2 lemon*
*salt*
*freshly-ground black pepper*
*extra lemon wedges to garnish*

Grease a shallow, ovenproof dish and, if it has no lid, cut a piece of foil to cover it.

Split each herring right through and, without removing the tail, take out the backbone. Sprinkle with the juice of 1/2 lemon and season well with salt and pepper.

To make the stuffing, melt the butter in a small pan and fry the onion over moderate heat for 4 minutes. Add the mushrooms and continue frying for a further 3 minutes. Remove the pan from the heat, stir in the chopped watercress and the grated zest of $\frac{1}{2}$ lemon. Season with salt and pepper. Spread the stuffing inside each fish and fold back to enclose it.

Place the fish in the ovenproof dish, cover and cook at 180°C(350°F)/Gas 4 for 30 minutes, until they are cooked through.

To make the sauce, combine the yoghurt with the chopped watercress and grated zest and strained juice of $\frac{1}{2}$ lemon and season well.

Garnish the cooked fish with watercress sprigs and lemon wedges and serve the sauce separately.

*Serves 4*

## Herrings with Cucumber Stuffing

The piquant yoghurt sauce offsets the richness of the fish and brings out the subtle flavour of the lemon and cucumber filling.

*4 herrings, heads removed, and cleaned*
*1 lemon*
*salt*
*freshly-ground black pepper*
*15 g ($\frac{1}{2}$ oz) butter*
*1 small onion, skinned and finely chopped*
*12.5-cm (5-in) length cucumber, chopped but not peeled*
*50 g (2 oz) breadcrumbs*
*1 egg, beaten*
*2 tablespoons fresh chopped parsley*

For sauce
*150 ml (5 fl oz) natural yoghurt*
*1 teaspoon lemon juice*
*grated zest of 1 lemon*
*7.5-cm (3-in) length cucumber, chopped*
*salt*
*freshly-ground black pepper*
*1 tablespoon fresh chopped chives*
*lemon and cucumber slices to garnish*

Grease a shallow, ovenproof dish and, if it has no lid, cut a piece of foil large enough to cover it.

Split down both sides of each herring, using a small, sharp knife. Remove the backbone, but take care not to remove the tail. Sprinkle the flesh with the lemon juice and season with salt and pepper.

To make the stuffing, melt the butter in a small pan, add the onion and cucumber and fry gently for 5 minutes, stirring occasionally. Remove the pan from the heat and stir in the grated zest of the lemon, the breadcrumbs, beaten egg and parsley, and season with salt and pepper. Mix well, divide the stuffing between the 4 herrings, pat it down evenly and 'close up' the herrings.

Place the fish in the ovenproof dish, cover and cook at 180°C(350°F)/Gas 4 for 30 minutes, until the herrings are tender.

To make the sauce, combine the ingredients listed, reserving a little of the chopped chives for garnish.

Garnish the cooked herrings with lemon and cucumber slices and sprinkle with chives. Serve the sauce separately. New potatoes and whole green beans are good accompaniments for lunch or supper.
*Serves 4*

## Haddock and Mushroom Casserole
A perfect think-ahead dish which will wait quite happily all day or overnight until you are ready to cook it.

*25 g (1 oz) butter*
*50 g (2 oz) mushrooms, wiped and sliced*
*1 small green pepper, de-seeded and sliced*
*3 eggs*
*150 ml (¼ pint) milk*
*75 g (3 oz) fresh white breadcrumbs*
*225 g (8 oz) smoked haddock, cooked and flaked*
*350 g (12 oz) yoghurt cheese (see page 5)*
*salt*
*freshly-ground black pepper*
*1 tablespoon chives, finely chopped or cut*

Grease a 1.25-litre (2-pint) shallow casserole.

Melt the butter in a small pan and fry the mushrooms over moderate heat for 3–4 minutes, then drain. Reserve a few mushroom slices and strips of green pepper for garnish. Dice the remaining green pepper, fry it in the pan for 2–3 minutes, and drain. Beat the eggs and milk together, pour on to the breadcrumbs and leave to soak for 10 minutes. Add all the remaining ingredients, mix well and taste for seasoning, adding more if necessary. Turn the mixture into the prepared casserole, arrange the mushroom and pepper slices on top and stand the casserole in a roasting tin of warm water. Bake at 180°C(350°F)/Gas 4 for 45–50 minutes, until the mixture is firmly set.
*Serves 4*

## Cheese and Watercress Croquettes
The croquettes can be prepared the night before, ready to fry in the morning. The basic paste of thick white sauce and mashed potato can be flavoured in numerous ways – with diced cooked chicken or ham, flaked cooked fish, chopped mushrooms or crisply fried bacon.

*25 g (1 oz) butter*
*25 g (1 oz) flour*

*150 ml (¹/₄ pint) milk, hot*
*450 g (1 lb) cooked potatoes, mashed with 25 g (1 oz) butter and 2 tablespoons*
*natural yoghurt*
*75 g (3 oz) cheese, grated*
*1 bunch watercress, washed and picked over*
*salt*
*freshly-ground black pepper*
*1 egg, beaten*
*fresh breadcrumbs*
*fat or oil for frying*

Melt the butter in a medium-sized pan, stir in the flour then gradually add the milk, stirring until a roux is formed. Add the mashed potato and cheese and mix thoroughly. Blanch the watercress in boiling, salted water for 1 minute, drain well and chop. Add the watercress to the potato mixture and season well with salt and pepper. This is the time to stir in any other ingredients you might like to use for flavouring, as noted above.

Flour your hands and form the mixture into 8 sausage shapes. Dip the croquettes into the beaten egg, then coat with breadcrumbs.

Heat the fat or oil in a frying pan and, when smoking hot, add the croquettes. Fry, turning once, until they are crisp and golden brown all over.

These croquettes are good with cold ham or grilled bacon.

### Cod Crispies

The fish chunks can be served with a plain yoghurt dressing for breakfast. And later in the day, even for a party, dressed up with a paprika dip. Other firm white fish such as haddock or coley fillet can be used instead.

*900 g (2 lb) fresh cod, haddock or coley fillet*

For marinade
*2 tablespoons olive oil*
*2 tablespoons lemon juice*
*salt*
*freshly-ground black pepper*

For batter
*100 g (4 oz) flour*
*¹/₂ teaspoon salt*
*1 egg*
*250 ml (scant ¹/₂ pint) water*

For dip (optional)
*1 small onion, skinned and finely chopped*
*3 teaspoons lemon juice*

*150 ml (5 fl oz) natural yoghurt, whipped*
*salt*
*scant 1/2 teaspoon paprika pepper*

*oil for frying (see method)*
*4 rashers streaky bacon, de-rinded, chopped and crisply fried, to*
*garnish*

Skin the fish and cut the fillets into chunks about 3.5 cm (1½ ins) square. Put the fish in a shallow dish, mix together the marinade ingredients, spoon over the fish and cover. Leave in the refrigerator or a cool place, stirring occasionally, for 2–3 hours, or longer if convenient.

To make the batter, whisk together the flour, salt, egg and water in a small basin until the batter is smooth.

If you want to prepare the dip, stir the chopped onion and the lemon juice into the whipped yoghurt and season with salt and paprika pepper. Chill in a covered container until needed.

To cook the fish, heat the oil to a depth of about 3.5 cm (1½ in) in a pan until just smoking. Pat the fish chunks dry on kitchen paper and dip them a few at a time in the batter, shaking off any excess. Fry the fish pieces a few at a time for about 5 minutes, turning once. When the fish is cooked and the batter crisp, remove with a draining spoon and drain on crumpled kitchen paper. Keep hot while you fry the remaining fish.

Pile the fish on to a hot serving dish and sprinkle with the bacon snippets. If serving the dip, provide skewers for dipping the hot fish into the cold sauce.
*Serves 6–8*


## Dutch Cheese Pie
Caraway pastry is a perfect foundation for this melting, gooey cheese and yoghurt filling.

*175 g (6 oz) flour*
*pinch salt*
*1 teaspoon caraway seeds*
*75 g (3 oz) butter*

For filling
*50 g (2 oz) breadcrumbs*
*100 g (4 oz) ham, finely chopped*
*225 g (8 oz) Gouda cheese, grated*
*3 eggs, lightly beaten*
*1/2 teaspoon caraway seeds*
*1/2 teaspoon made mustard*
*150 ml (5 fl oz) natural yoghurt*

Grease a 20-cm (8-in) flan case.

Sift the flour and salt together in a bowl, stir in the caraway seeds and rub in the butter until the mixture resembles fine breadcrumbs. Mix to a stiff dough with a little cold water and knead lightly until smooth. Roll out on a lightly-floured board, use to line the flan case, and leave in the refrigerator or a cold place for about 20 minutes. Line the pastry case with foil and fill with 'baking beans'. Bake 'blind' at 200°C(400°F)/Gas 6 for 10–15 minutes, until the pastry is set. Remove from the oven, tip the baking beans back into a jar, remove the foil and leave the pastry to cool.

Mix together the ingredients for the filling, pour into the flan case and bake at 180°C(350°F)/Gas 4 for 30–40 minutes, until the filling is well risen and golden brown. Serve hot.
*Serves 4–6*

**Cheese and Vegetable Flan**
Fresh garden vegetables combine delightfully with a cheesy egg custard in a colourful flan.

For cheese pastry
*175 g (6 oz) flour*
*½ teaspoon salt*
*75 g (3 oz) butter* or *margarine*
*75 g (3 oz) Cheddar cheese, finely grated*
*3 tablespoons water*

For filling
*175 g (6 oz) yoghurt cheese (see page 5)*
*2 eggs, beaten*
*300 ml (½ pint) milk*
*salt*
*freshly-ground black pepper*
*450 g (1 lb) freshly cooked mixed vegetables (see method)*

Grease a 25-cm (10-in) flan ring.

To make the pastry, sift the flour and salt into a bowl and rub in the fat until the mixture resembles fine breadcrumbs. Stir in the cheese and add the water, mixing with a spatula, to make a stiff dough. Chill the dough in the refrigerator for 30 minutes. On a lightly-floured board, roll the pastry into a circle about 35 cm (14 ins) in diameter. Carefully lift this on to the flan case and trim the edges. Line the pastry case with foil and fill with dried beans kept specially for the purpose ('baking beans'). Bake the pastry case 'blind' (without the filling) at 200°C(400°F)/Gas 6 for 15 minutes. Remove from the oven, tip the baking beans into a jar for further use, and peel off the foil.

To make the filling, beat the yoghurt cheese until smooth, then gradually beat in the eggs and milk, a little at a time. Season well with salt and pepper.

30

Choose vegetables according to season – a mixture from new potatoes, carrots, peas, broad beans, French beans, cauliflower, mushrooms, courgettes – and cook them in boiling, salted water until they are barely tender. Cut them into slices, divide the cauliflower into florets, and arrange them in a pattern in the partly-cooked flan case. Pour over the custard mixture, sprinkle with black pepper and return to the oven. Bake for about 30–35 minutes, until the filling has set and the top is golden brown.
*Serves 6*

## Upside-down Cheese Scone

The colourful topping of onion rings, tomato slices and black olives gives this dish a pizza look. You can make it more substantial by adding strips of ham, salami, anchovy or cheese.

*25 g (1 oz) butter*
*1 medium-sized onion, skinned and cut into rings*
*3 large tomatoes, skinned and sliced*
*salt*
*freshly-ground black pepper*

For scone
*225 g (8 oz) self-raising flour*
*1/4 teaspoon salt*
*50 g (2 oz) soft margarine*
*100 g (4 oz) yoghurt cheese (see page 5)*
*1 egg*
*2 tablespoons milk*

For garnish
*4 black olives, stoned*

Grease a 20-cm (8-in) sandwich tin and line the base with a circle of greased greaseproof paper.

Melt the butter in a pan and fry the onion rings over a moderate heat for 5 minutes, until they begin to turn. colour. Stir them with a wooden spoon occasionally. Arrange the onion slices in the sandwich tin and cover them with circles of the tomato slices. Season with salt and pepper (be sparing with the salt, or omit it entirely, if you choose to add ham or anchovies to the topping).

To make the scone dough, sift together the flour and salt and rub in the margarine. Stir in the yoghurt cheese. Beat the egg and milk together, add to the flour mixture and stir to make a soft dough. Knead lightly on a floured board and roll out to make a 20-cm (8-in) circle. Press the dough into the sandwich tin, pushing it lightly against the rim. Bake in a pre-heated oven at 220°C(425°F)/Gas 7 for 20–25 minutes until the scone is risen and brown. Turn out of the tin on to a serving plate, garnish with the olives and serve hot.
*Serves 4–6*

## Watercress Flan

Nuts and crisp vegetables creamed together with yoghurt cheese make a lovely filling for a cold flan.

*100 g (4 oz) flour*
*pinch salt*
*25 g (1 oz) butter*
*25 g (1 oz) lard*
*cayenne pepper*
*50 g (2 oz) Cheddar cheese, grated*
*2 tablespoons water*

For filling
*100 g (4 oz) yoghurt cheese (see page 5)*
*50 g (2 oz) walnuts, chopped*
*¹/₂ medium-sized cucumber, chopped*
*1 bunch watercress, washed, picked over and chopped (reserve a*
  *few sprigs to garnish)*
*50 g (2 oz) mushrooms, wiped and chopped*
*4 stalks celery, washed and chopped*

Grease a 20-cm (8-in) flan ring.

To make the cheese pastry, sift the flour and salt together in a bowl and rub in the fats until the mixture resembles fine breadcrumbs. Stir in a good pinch of cayenne pepper, then the grated cheese. Bind the mixture with the water and form into a ball. Wrap this loosely in foil and leave to rest in the refrigerator or a cool place for at least 30 minutes. Roll out the pastry, lift into the flan case, trim the edges and line the case with foil. Fill with 'baking beans' and bake 'blind' at 180°C(350°F)/Gas 4 for 30 minutes, removing the foil for the last 5 minutes to dry the pastry top.

To make the filling, put the yoghurt cheese in a bowl and add the chopped walnuts, cucumber, watercress, mushrooms and celery. Season well with salt and a little cayenne pepper. If the mixture is too stiff, soften it with natural yoghurt or 1 tablespoon milk.

When the flan case has cooled, remove it from the ring and put it on to a serving plate. Spread the cheese mixture into the case, sprinkle with a pinch of cayenne pepper and garnish with the reserve sprigs of watercress.
*Serves 4–6*

## Bruncheon Sandwiches

Open sandwiches are good for breakfast. They look tempting enough to delight people who don't have much of an appetite in the morning, and can be concocted from all the tasty pieces of cheese, meat and vegetables in the refrigerator.

For each sandwich, you will need 1 slice of white bread, buttered, *or* pumpernickel, *or* rye bread, *or* wholemeal bread; a variety of breads makes for a more interesting selection of sandwiches. Cover each slice of bread with a slice of ham, salami, mortadella, liver sausage, thinly-sliced cheese or thinly-sliced smoked mackerel or herring.

Decorate some sandwiches with a teaspoon of yoghurt cheese mixed with walnuts and seedless raisins; with whipped yoghurt stirred with capers and chopped onion; or with whipped yoghurt and sweetcorn kernels spiced with finely-chopped red or green peppers.

The final garnish is all-important. Cut thin slices of lemon, cucumber, carrot, hard-boiled egg, and spread them in a fan shape; cut onion rings; 'lily' shapes from radishes; star shapes from slices of green and red pepper; arrange orange or tangerine segments butterfly fashion.

You can prepare the fillings and garnishes in advance and keep them in covered containers in the refrigerator ready to assemble in time for lunch.

## Smoked Haddock Mousse
Using boil-in-the-bag haddock makes this mousse easier to prepare – and doesn't leave the kitchen with a legacy of fish smells!

*1 215-g (7-oz) packet buttered smoked haddock fillets*
*300 ml (10 fl oz) natural yoghurt*
*2 eggs, hard boiled and shelled*
*½ bunch watercress, washed and 'picked over'*
*grated zest and juice of ½ lemon*
*2 teaspoons gelatine*
*2 tablespoons water*
*salt*
*freshly-ground black pepper*

Cook the smoked haddock fillets according to the instructions on the packet. Remove the fish from the bag, reserving the liquor. Skin and flake the fish very finely and mix it with the yoghurt and one chopped hard-boiled egg. Reserving a few sprigs of watercress, chop the rest and add to the fish mixture with the grated lemon zest. Sprinkle the gelatine over the lemon juice and water in a small bowl. Stand it in a pan of hot water to dissolve, and when it is cool, stir into the fish mixture with the reserved fish liquor. Season well and pour into a 600-ml (1-pint) soufflé dish. Chill until set. Garnish with slices of the remaining hard-boiled egg and the watercress sprigs.
*Serves 4*

## Courgette Ring Mould
An attractive dish for summer brunch or supper, and appealingly economical when courgettes are in season.

*300 ml (1/2 pint) milk*
*1 bayleaf*
*1 sprig thyme*
*1 sprig parsley*
*1 small onion, skinned and halved*
*275 g (10 oz) yoghurt cheese (see page 5)*
*1 1/2 tablespoons Bordeaux mustard*
*juice of 1/2 lemon*
*150 ml (5 fl oz) mayonnaise*
*20 g (3/4 oz) powdered gelatine*
*3 tablespoons water*
*225 g (8 oz) courgettes, washed and trimmed*
*150 ml (5 fl oz) natural yoghurt, whipped*
*2 egg whites, stiffly beaten*
*salt*
*cayenne pepper*
*1 tablespoon fresh chopped parsley*

Put the milk, bayleaf, herbs and onion in a pan and bring slowly to the boil. Remove from the heat, cover and leave for 20 minutes for the flavours to infuse. In a large bowl, mix together the yoghurt cheese, mustard and lemon juice. Stir in the mayonnaise and then gradually mix in the strained milk, pouring it on slowly as the rest of the mixture absorbs it. Dissolve the gelatine in the water in a small bowl in a pan of hot water.

Cut the courgettes into small cubes and blanch them in boiling, salted water for 2 minutes. Drain them and leave to cool. When the courgettes are cool, stir them into the cheese mixture, then gradually pour on the gelatine, stirring all the time. Leave in a cool place until just beginning to set, then fold in the whipped yoghurt and stiffly-beaten egg whites. Season with salt and a pinch of cayenne pepper, and stir in the chopped parsley. Rinse a 1.5-litre (2 1/2-pint) ring mould in cold water and pour in the mixture. Leave in the refrigerator or a cold place to set.

To turn out the mould, dip in hot water for 2–3 seconds and invert on to a serving dish. Garnish with herbs, slices of tomato or lemon, as you wish.
*Serves 6*

## Blue Cheese Ring

This savoury is more in the brunch or supper category, with a memorably strong flavour. It is also ideal to serve at the end of a dinner party.

*15 g (1/2 oz) powdered gelatine*
*3 tablespoons hot water*
*100 g (4 oz) Danish blue cheese*
*150 ml (5 fl oz) natural yoghurt, whipped*
*50 g (2 oz) walnuts, chopped*

*2 eggs, separated*
*2 tablespoons tomato ketchup*
*15 g (¹/₂ oz) whole walnuts, to garnish*
*6–8 black olives, to garnish*

Dissolve the gelatine in the water, in a small bowl standing in a pan of hot water. Set aside to cool.

Crumble the cheese and mix it with the whipped yoghurt, chopped walnuts, beaten egg yolks and tomato ketchup. Pour on the cooled gelatine, stirring all the time, then fold in the stiffly-beaten egg whites.

Rinse a 900-ml (1¹/₂-pint) mould in cold water, then pour in the cheese mixture. Set aside in the refrigerator or in a cold place to set. Turn the mould out on to a serving plate and decorate it with whole walnuts and black olives. For a more substantial dish, pile a celery and apple salad into the centre of the mould.
*Serves 4–6*

## Prawn and Cheese Mousse

A creamy mousse that is perfect for a picnic, brunch or supper, or as a first course for a dinner party.

*15 g (¹/₂ oz) butter*
*15 g (¹/₂ oz) flour*
*300 ml (¹/₂ pint) dry cider (reserve 3 tablespoons)*
*225 g (8 oz) yoghurt cheese (see page 5)*
*2 eggs, separated*
*2 tablespoons tomato ketchup*
*2 tablespoons fresh chopped parsley*
*salt*
*freshly-ground black pepper*
*225 g (8 oz) prawns, chopped (reserve 4)*
*15 g (¹/₂ oz) powdered gelatine*
*150 ml (5 fl oz) natural yoghurt, whipped*

Melt the butter in a small pan, add the flour and cook, stirring, for 1 minute. Remove from the heat and gradually stir in the cider. Return the pan to the heat, stirring, and cook for 1 minute. Remove the pan from the heat. Add the yoghurt cheese, egg yolks, tomato ketchup and parsley and season with salt and pepper. Stir until the cheese has blended, then add the prawns.

Pour the reserved 3 tablespoons cider into a small bowl, sprinkle on the gelatine and stand in a pan of hot water, stirring to dissolve. Set aside to cool.

Stir the yoghurt into the cheese mixture, then gradually pour in the gelatine and cider, stirring all the time. Stiffly beat the egg whites and fold them into the mixture, using a metal spoon.

Rinse a 1-litre (2-pint) mould in cold water, then pour in the cheese mixture.

Leave in the refrigerator or a cold place to set. Dip in hot water for 2–3 seconds and invert on to a serving plate. Garnish with the reserved prawns. Serve with rye bread or pumpernickel for an effective contrast of textures and flavours.
*Serves 8*


## Pasta Salad
Few of us would consider eating spaghetti first thing in the morning. But pasta salad is a different matter altogether, and makes a super brunch dish.

*75 g (3 oz) short-cut pasta such as shells, wheels or macaroni*
*2 dessert apples*
*1 tablespoon lemon juice*
*2 stalks celery, washed and chopped*
*1 tablespoon seedless raisins*
*salt*
*freshly-ground black pepper*
*2 heaped tablespoons mayonnaise*
*2 tablespoons natural yoghurt*
*1 tablespoon walnuts, roughly chopped*

Cook the pasta as directed on the packet, drain and refresh in cold water. Drain thoroughly.

Core the apples, without peeling them, chop them into dice and toss them in the lemon juice to preserve their colour. Turn the drained pasta into a large bowl and mix in the apple, celery and raisins. Season with salt and pepper and stir in the mayonnaise and yoghurt. Turn into a salad bowl and sprinkle with the chopped walnuts.

This salad is very good with cold Continental-type sausage, such as salami.
*Serves 4*


## Cheese Roulade
Yoghurt cheese and crisply fried bacon make the soft but crunchy filling for this cheese and spinach roll. It's rather a showy dish, and could well be served not only for lunch or supper but on a picnic, or as the first course at a dinner party.

*3 eggs*
*pinch salt*
*75 g (3 oz) flour*
*100 g (4 oz) Cheddar cheese, grated*
*450 g (1 lb) spinach, cooked, drained and sieved*
*225 g (8 oz) yoghurt cheese (see page 5)*
*5 tablespoons natural yoghurt*
*salt*

*freshly-ground black pepper*
*100 g (4 oz) bacon, chopped and crisply fried*

Grease a Swiss roll tin and line it with greased greaseproof paper.

Whisk together the eggs and salt until thick and creamy. Using a metal spoon, and light, quick movements, fold in the flour, then the grated cheese and the spinach. Spread the mixture at once over the prepared tin and bake in a pre-heated oven at 220°C(425°F)/Gas 7 for 12–15 minutes, until it is set.

Turn the sponge on to a piece of greased greaseproof paper and carefully peel the paper from the base. Trim the edges to neaten the shape and then roll it up loosely, with a piece of greaseproof paper inside. Leave until cold.

Beat together the yoghurt cheese and the yoghurt and season well. Unroll the sponge, remove the greaseproof paper, spread the sponge with the cheese mixture and sprinkle with bacon. Roll up again, wrap it loosely in foil and leave in the refrigerator or a cool place to rest before slicing.
*Serves 6*

CHAPTER FOUR

# *Tea by the Fire*

In Victorian times, afternoon tea was a daily event in the social calendar, when ladies exchanged gentle gossip over a trolley laden with genteel sandwiches, caraway cake, gingerbread and Victoria sponges. Nursery tea was, of course, taken elsewhere, and was even more substantial.

Nowadays, whether it is taken by the fire, in the warm and friendly atmosphere of the kitchen, or in the garden on a summer's day, tea can be the most homely meal of all. It is the time for an outburst of news and confidences as the children come rushing home from school; a time, perhaps, to rest on one's laurels for a while, when most of the day's housework is done; and for others, who work away from home during the week-days, a time of blissful leisure to be tasted only at the weekends.

The size of the meal can vary from a piece of cake and a biscuit, when there is a main meal to come in the evening, to a full-scale affair that keeps hunger pangs at bay until breakfast the next day. The family timetable will decide how great a selection of sandwiches and scones, cakes and teabreads is offered at a sitting, and whether light savoury dishes, such as those in Chapter 3, are added.

Many of these tea-time recipes are 'good keepers' and some, the moist teabreads and cakes, actually improve by being kept in a tin for a day or two, while the flavours blend and mellow.

Some of the recipes will seem familiar; and certainly the methods are standard and simple. But see what a noticeable difference the inclusion of yoghurt makes; what a lighter, fresher texture and flavour it can bring to tea-time baking.

## Date and Walnut Loaf

I served this fruit loaf to a family of weekend guests one November, before the bonfire party. They asked me to make another one, and leave it in the oven while they let off their fireworks!

225 g (8 oz) self-raising flour
1/4 teaspoon salt
1/2 teaspoon ground mixed spice
50 g (2 oz) butter
50 g (2 oz) sugar
100 g (4 oz) dates, stoned and chopped
75 g (3 oz) walnuts, chopped (reserve a few halves to decorate)
1 egg
150 ml (5 fl oz) natural yoghurt

For icing
75 g (3 oz) icing sugar, sifted
2 drops cinnamon essence
1 tablespoon water

Grease a 450-g (1-lb) loaf tin.

Sift together the flour, salt and mixed spice and rub in the butter until the mixture resembles fine breadcrumbs. Stir in the sugar, dates and walnuts. Beat the egg and yoghurt together and stir into the dry ingredients. Beat thoroughly for 1 minute. Turn the mixture into the greased loaf tin and bake at 180°C(350°F)/Gas 4 for 1 hour 5 minutes, until the loaf is golden brown. Leave in the tin to cool for a few minutes, then turn on to a wire rack.

To make the icing, sift the icing sugar into a bowl, add the cinnamon essence and water and mix to a smooth consistency. Spread the icing over the cake when it is cold, and decorate with the reserved walnut halves.

*Serves 8*

## Banana and Raisin Teabread

The use of wholemeal flour makes this teabread appetizingly rich in colour. Make it three or four days before serving – it improves with keeping.

50 g (2 oz) margarine
3 tablespoons clear honey
275 g (10 oz) self-raising wholemeal flour
1 1/2 teaspoons baking powder
1/2 teaspoon salt
50 g (2 oz) soft dark brown sugar
100 g (4 oz) seedless raisins
3 small bananas, mashed
1 egg
150 ml (5 fl oz) natural yoghurt

Grease a 450-g (1-lb) loaf tin.

Put the margarine and honey into a pan and heat until the fat has melted. Mix together the flour, baking powder and salt in a bowl and stir in the sugar, raisins and mashed banana. Beat the egg and yoghurt together and add to the dry mixture with the honey and margarine. Beat the mixture well for 1 minute.

Pour into the prepared loaf tin and bake at 180°C(350°F)/Gas 4 for 1 hour, until the teabread is well risen and golden brown, and beginning to shrink away from the sides of the tin.

Store in a tin for 3–4 days and serve sliced and buttered.
*Serves 8*

## Banana Cake
Delicious as banana sandwiches drenched in sugar – a moist, rich cake with a lemony icing.

*100 g (4 oz) butter*
*150 g (5 oz) caster sugar*
*1 egg, beaten*
*3 bananas, mashed*
*200 g (7 oz) self-raising flour*
*1/2 teaspoon bicarbonate of soda*
*1 tablespoon natural yoghurt*

For icing
*100 g (4 oz) icing sugar*
*juice of 1/2 lemon*
*1 tablespoon water*
*lemon slices to decorate (optional)*

Grease a 20-cm (8-in) sandwich tin.

Cream together the butter and sugar, then gradually beat in the egg and mashed banana. Sift together the flour and bicarbonate of soda and fold into the mixture. Beat in the yoghurt to give a soft, dropping consistency.

Turn the mixture into the prepared tin and bake at 150°C(300°F)/Gas 2 for 1 hour, until the cake is firm. Remove from the oven and when the cake is nearly cold, turn out on to a wire rack.

To make the icing, sift the icing sugar into a bowl and mix with the lemon juice and enough water to make it spreadable. Spread the glacé icing over the cake when it is cold. Decorate, if liked, with lemon slices or crystallized fruit slices.
*Serves 8*

## Apple Cake
Cheese and apples are always perfect partners. Here, a soft, lemony cheese topping decorates a moist fruit cake.

100 g (4 oz) self-raising flour
1/2 teaspoon salt
1 teaspoon ground cinnamon
1/2 teaspoon ground mixed spice
40 g (1 1/2 oz) margarine
50 g (2 oz) caster sugar
50 g (2 oz) soft brown sugar
1 egg, beaten
180 ml (6 fl oz) apple purée
50 g (2 oz) raisins
25 g (1 oz) walnuts, chopped

For topping
100 g (4 oz) icing sugar, sifted
100 g (4 oz) yoghurt cheese (see page 5)
grated rind and juice of 1 lemon
1 dessert apple to decorate
1 extra tablespoon lemon juice

Grease a cake tin 18 cm (7 in) square.

Sift together the flour, salt and spices. In another bowl beat the margarine and sugars together until light and creamy. Gradually beat in the egg, then fold in the sifted flour mixture alternately with the apple purée. Beat well, then stir in the raisins and chopped walnuts.

Turn the mixture into the prepared tin and bake at 180°C(350°F)/Gas 4 for 45–50 minutes, until the cake is firm. Allow to cool in the tin, then turn the cake on to a wire rack.

To make the topping, beat together the sifted icing sugar and the yoghurt cheese, then beat in the lemon rind and juice. Spread the mixture evenly over the top of the cake and make a tram-line pattern with a fork. Cut the dessert apple across into slices, without peeling or coring it, so that the slices show the radiating pattern on the core in cross-section. Dip them in the lemon juice, then arrange the slices overlapping in a line down the centre of the cake.
*Serves 8*

## Apricot Cake

This is a 'one-step' cake, no rubbing in, creaming or whisking. Just give it one jolly good beating to show who's boss!

225 g (8 oz) self-raising wholemeal flour
150 g (5 oz) soft dark brown sugar
150 g (5 oz) soft margarine
2 eggs
100 g (4 oz) dried apricots, chopped

41

*50 g (2 oz) sultanas*
*175 g (6 oz) raisins*
*50 g (2 oz) walnuts, chopped*
*120 ml (4 fl oz) natural yoghurt*

Grease a deep 18-cm (7-in) cake tin and line it with greased greaseproof paper.

Mix the flour and sugar well together in a large bowl, then add the margarine and eggs. Beat well, then add the dried fruit and nuts and lastly the yoghurt. Beat thoroughly until the mixture is smooth. Turn it into the prepared tin and bake at 150°C(300°F)/Gas 2 for 2 hours until the cake is firm and has slightly shrunk away from the edge of the tin. Leave in the tin to cool for 20 minutes, then turn the cake on to a wire rack to become cold. Store in an airtight tin.
*Serves 8*

## Sticky-top Brown Cake
There's sugar and spice, nuts and chocolate, in this moist cake covered with boiled frosting.

*100 g (4 oz) margarine*
*175 g (6 oz) caster sugar*
*3 eggs, beaten*
*225 g (8 oz) flour*
*1 teaspoon bicarbonate of soda*
*1 teaspoon baking powder*
*1/2 teaspoon salt*
*1/2 teaspoon ground cinnamon*
*150 ml (5 fl oz) natural yoghurt*
*50 g (2 oz) chocolate chips*
*50 g (2 oz) hazelnuts, chopped*

For topping
*50 g (2 oz) flour*
*1 teaspoon ground cinnamon*
*25 g (1 oz) butter*
*50 g (2 oz) soft light brown sugar*

For frosting
*50 g (2 oz) icing sugar, sifted*
*50 g (2 oz) butter*
*2 tablespoons milk*
*few drops cinnamon essence*

Grease a 20-cm (8-in) cake tin.

Cream together the margarine and caster sugar in a large bowl and gradually add the beaten eggs. Add a little of the measured flour if the mixture begins to curdle. Sift the flour, soda, baking powder, salt and ground cinnamon together and stir into the creamed mixture alternately with the yoghurt. Stir in the chocolate chips and chopped hazelnuts and blend well. Turn the mixture into the prepared tin. Sprinkle on the topping and bake at 180°C(350°F)/Gas 4 for 1 hour 10 minutes, until the cake is firm.

To make the topping, sift together the flour and cinnamon, rub in the butter and stir in the sugar. Sprinkle over the cake before it is cooked.

To make the frosting, put the 4 ingredients into a small pan and stir until the butter has melted and the sugar dissolved. Bring to the boil and simmer for 3 minutes. Pour over the hot cake as soon as it is taken from the oven. Leave the cake to cool in the tin and the frosting to set hard.
*Serves 8*

## Malt Sandwich Cake

This malt cake is not the conventional one made in a loaf tin and buttered. It is made in sandwich tins and filled with a malty butter cream. Needless to say, it is very rich.

*100 g (4 oz) flour*
*75 g (3 oz) malted milk powder*
*100 g (4 oz) butter*
*100 g (4 oz) caster sugar*
*2 eggs*
*2 tablespoons natural yoghurt*

For filling and topping
*75 g (3 oz) butter*
*175 g (6 oz) icing sugar*
*50 g (2 oz) malted milk powder*
*few drops vanilla essence*
*1–2 tablespoons milk*
*25 g (1 oz) walnuts, chopped (reserve a few halves to decorate)*

Grease 2 18-cm (7-in) sandwich tins.

To make the cake, sift together the flour and malted milk powder into a bowl. In another bowl cream together the butter and sugar until light and fluffy. Gradually beat in the eggs alternately with the flour mixture. Beat well, then beat in the yoghurt. The mixture should be a soft dropping consistency. Turn the mixture into the prepared tins and level the surface with a knife. Bake at 190°C(375°F)/Gas 5 for 20 minutes until the cakes are risen and firm. Allow to cool in the tins for 5 minutes, then turn on to a wire rack.

To make the filling, cream the butter in a bowl, then gradually beat in the icing sugar, malted milk powder and vanilla essence. Add just enough milk to make the mixture spreadable without being runny. Stir in the chopped walnuts.

Spread half the filling on one sandwich cake, cover with the other and spread the remaining butter cream on top. Make a trellis pattern with a fork and decorate with the reserved walnut halves.
*Serves 8*

## Light Fruit Cake

When you've made yoghurt cheese and creamed off all the curds, what do you do with the whey? Here's one answer – it gives lightness to this favourite tuck-box cake.

*450 g (1 lb) flour, sieved*
*225 g (8 oz) margarine*
*225 g (8 oz) caster sugar*
*100 g (4 oz) raisins*
*100 g (4 oz) sultanas*
*50 g (2 oz) currants*
*50 g (2 oz) mixed candied peel, chopped*
*1 egg*
*180 ml (6 fl oz) whey (see page 5; or you can use half milk and half water)*

Grease a deep 20-cm (8-in) cake tin.

Tip the sieved flour into a bowl and rub in the margarine until the mixture resembles fine breadcrumbs. Stir in the sugar and dried fruit and mix well. Beat together the egg and whey and gradually pour into the dry mixture, stir-beating with a wooden spoon.

Pour the mixture into the greased cake tin and bake at 180°C(350°F)/Gas 4 for 1½ hours. Leave the cake in the tin to cool a little, then turn it out to finish cooling on a wire rack. This cake keeps remarkably well in a tin.
*Serves 8–10*

## Spiced Fruit Cake

This is the kind of cake my grandmother used to call a 'keeping' cake – because it keeps well in a tin. But actually, with children around, it doesn't at all!

*275 g (10 oz) self-raising flour*
*½ teaspoon mixed spice*
*½ teaspoon ground cinnamon*
*175 g (6 oz) margarine*
*150 g (5 oz) soft light brown sugar*
*225 g (8 oz) raisins*
*50 g (2 oz) mixed candied peel, chopped*
*50 g (2 oz) walnuts, chopped*
*2 eggs*
*3 tablespoons natural yoghurt*

Grease a 20-cm (8-in) cake tin and line it with greased greaseproof paper.

Sift together the flour and spices and rub in the margarine. Stir in the sugar, raisins, chopped peel and walnuts. Beat together the eggs and yoghurt and beat into the mixture. Pour the mixture into the lined cake tin and bake at 180°C(350°F)/Gas 4 for 1½–1¾ hours. Allow the cake to cool in the tin for a few minutes before turning it out on to a wire rack.
*Serves 10*

## Easter Yoghurt Cake

Holiday times can bring a surfeit of richness, and anyway not everyone likes fruit cake. Here's a plain cake, sharpened with candied peel and lemon icing.

*100 g (4 oz) butter*
*175 g (6 oz) caster sugar*
*grated rind of 1 lemon*
*3 eggs, separated*
*175 g (6 oz) flour, sifted*
*180 ml (6 fl oz) natural yoghurt*
*50 g (2 oz) candied peel, chopped*

For icing
*100 g (4 oz) icing sugar, sifted*
*1 tablespoon lemon juice*
*a little water to mix*

Grease a 450-g (1-lb) loaf tin.

Cream the butter and sugar together in a bowl, add the lemon rind and beat well. Beat in the egg yolks one at a time and then add the sifted flour alternately with the yoghurt. Stir in the chopped peel. Whisk the egg whites until stiff and fold them into the mixture with a metal spoon. Turn into the prepared loaf tin and bake at 180°C(350°F)/Gas 4 for 1 hour, until the cake is well risen and golden brown. Turn out on to a wire rack to cool.

Put the icing sugar into a bowl with the lemon juice and add the water, a few drops at a time, until the icing is of a spreading consistency. When the cake is cold, dribble the lemon icing over the top.
*Serves 8*

## Danish Carrot Cake

A rich, moist slab cake with a smooth, creamy cheese topping that's as light as a snowflake.

*150 g (5 oz) Danish butter*
*200 g (7 oz) caster sugar*
*175 g (6 oz) carrots, peeled and finely grated*
*½ teaspoon salt*

*1 teaspoon ground cinnamon*
*2 large eggs, beaten*
*200 g (7 oz) flour*
*1 tablespoon baking powder*
*100 g (4 oz) seedless raisins*

For frosting
*50 g (2 oz) Danish butter, softened*
*100 g (4 oz) yoghurt cheese (see page 5)*
*100 g (4 oz) icing sugar, sifted*
*¹/₄ teaspoon vanilla essence*

Grease a baking tin 16 × 21 cm (6¹/₂ × 8 in).

Melt the butter over a low heat and pour it into a mixing bowl. Beat in the caster sugar, grated carrot, salt, ground cinnamon and eggs. Sift together the flour and baking powder and fold into the egg mixture a little at a time. Stir in the raisins and beat well. Pour the mixture into the prepared baking tin and bake at 170°C(325°F)/Gas 3 for 40–45 minutes. Test to see if the cake is cooked by pressing it with the fingertips. It should be firm to the touch. Allow the cake to cool in the tin for 5 minutes before turning it out on to a wire rack to become cold.

To make the frosting, beat together the softened butter and yoghurt cheese until completely smooth, then gradually beat in the sifted icing sugar and the vanilla essence. Spread the frosting evenly over the sides and top of the cake and scrape a lattice pattern over the surface with a fork.
*Serves 8*

## Sugar and Spice Ring
For a memorable showpiece, fill the centre of the spice ring with *pashka*, a Russian-inspired blend of yoghurt cheese and dried fruits, which you need to make the day before. More simply, the ring can be decorated with lemon icing.

*150 g (5 oz) margarine*
*50 g (2 oz) soft brown sugar*
*3 tablespoons clear honey*
*2 eggs*
*175 g (6 oz) self-raising flour*
*2 teaspoons mixed ground spice*
*¹/₂ teaspoon ground cinnamon*
*75 g (3 oz) walnuts, chopped*

For filling
*225 g (8 oz) yoghurt cheese (see page 5)*
*150 ml (5 oz) natural yoghurt*
*75 g (3 oz) caster sugar*
*50 g (2 oz) mixed candied peel, chopped*

46

*25 g (1 oz) blanched almonds, chopped*
*25 g (1 oz) seedless raisins*
*grated zest of ¹/₂ lemon*

Grease a 1.5-litre (2¹/₂-pint) ring mould.

To make the cake, cream the margarine, sugar and honey together in a bowl, then gradually beat in the eggs. Sieve the flour and spices and fold into the egg mixture with the walnuts. Pour into the prepared ring mould, level the surface and bake at 180°C(350°F)/Gas 4 for 40 minutes, until the cake is well risen. It should be firm to the touch and beginning to shrink from the edge of the mould. Allow the cake to cool in the mould before turning it out on to a wire rack to become cold.

To make the filling, beat together the yoghurt cheese, yoghurt and sugar, then mix in the chopped peel, almonds, raisins and lemon rind. Mix well. Line a small sieve with muslin and fill with the cheese mixture. Place a weight on top and leave over a bowl to drain for 24 hours.

Put the spice ring on to a serving plate or dish and spoon the *pashka* filling into the centre, forking up the surface into little peaks.

Serve any remaining *pashka* as a filling for wholemeal scones (see page 53).
*Serves 8*

## Turkish Yoghurt Cake

Reserve this moist, gooey cake for the avowed sweet-toothed – they'll love it. Serve it in small portions with the syrup and natural yoghurt spooned over.

*3 eggs*
*200 g (7 oz) sugar*
*225 ml (8 fl oz) natural yoghurt*
*225 g (8 oz) flour*
*1 teaspoon ground cinnamon*
*1 teaspoon bicarbonate of soda*
*juice of ¹/₂ lemon*

For syrup
*275 g (10 oz) sugar*
*225 ml (8 fl oz) water*
*natural yoghurt to serve*

Grease 2 450-g (1-lb) loaf tins.

Beat the eggs and sugar together in a bowl until the mixture is pale and creamy. Stir in the yoghurt. Sift the flour with the cinnamon and fold into the mixture. Stir well, then mix in the bicarbonate of soda and lemon juice – the mixture will froth a little at this stage.

Turn the mixture into the prepared tins and bake at 180°C(350°F)/Gas 4 for 35–40 minutes, until the cakes are well risen. Stand the tins on a wire rack and pour on the cooled syrup. The cakes will sink a little as they cool.

Make the syrup while the cakes are cooking, so that it has a chance to cool. Put the sugar and water into a small pan and stir until the sugar dissolves. Bring the syrup to the boil, then remove from the heat and allow to cool.

Serve one cake, cut in squares, at tea-time and the other with yoghurt spooned over, as a dessert. It is also perfect with vanilla ice-cream.
*Each cake serves 6–8*

## Sweet Fruit Muffins

Rich, sweet muffins, dark with brown sugar and raisins – the kind of baking that's a feature of health food restaurants and shops these days.

*225 g (8 oz) wholemeal flour*
*¼ teaspoon salt*
*3 teaspoons baking powder*
*50 g (2 oz) soft dark brown sugar*
*2 eggs*
*150 ml (¼ pint) natural yoghurt*
*4 tablespoons water*
*50 g (2 oz) raisins*
*25 g (1 oz) sultanas*
*25 g (1 oz) mixed candied peel, chopped*

Grease a tray of 12 deep patty tins.

Mix together the flour, salt, baking powder and sugar in a bowl and beat in the eggs. Whisk the yoghurt and water together and gradually add to the mixture, beating well. Stir in the dried fruit and beat again.

Spoon the batter into the greased patty tins. Bake near the top of the oven at 200°C(400°F)/Gas 6 for 12–15 minutes, until the muffins are well risen and golden brown.

Leave them to cool in the tins, then transfer them to a wire rack. Serve the same day, with unsalted butter.
*Makes 12 muffins*

## Pumpkin Muffins

Some pumpkins are so large that one wonders how to cook all that deliciously flame-coloured flesh in a number of interesting ways. These muffins, spiced and golden, are one light-as-a-feather solution.

*175 g (6 oz) pumpkin, skin and seeds removed*
*1 egg*
*120 ml (4 fl oz) natural yoghurt*
*40 g (1½ oz) white vegetable fat, melted*
*175 g (6 oz) self-raising flour*
*100 g (4 oz) caster sugar*
*½ teaspoon ground cinnamon*

*¹/₂ teaspoon ground mixed spice*
*50 g (2 oz) seedless raisins*
*25 g (1 oz) sultanas*

Grease a tray of 12 deep patty tins.

Cook the pumpkin in a very little water, or steam it over a pan of boiling water, until it is tender. Drain, mash it thoroughly and allow to cool.

In a bowl, beat together the egg and yoghurt and stir in the cooled, melted fat and the pumpkin purée. Sift together the flour, sugar and spices and stir into the pumpkin mixture. Do not worry that the batter is a little lumpy. Stir in the dried fruit and blend well.

Spoon the mixture into the prepared patty tins and bake at 200°C(400°F)/Gas 6 for 20–25 minutes, until the muffins are well risen and golden brown. Allow them to cool a little in the pans, then turn them on to a wire rack. They are delicious served warm with butter, or cold with butter and apple jam.
*Makes 12 muffins*


## Gingerbread

I like to have a slab of gingerbread maturing in a tin for a day or two before any long holiday weekend. It gives one a sense of security to be able to produce it, all moist and glistening, at a moment's notice when the doorbell rings.

*100 g (4 oz) butter*
*50 g (2 oz) soft dark brown sugar*
*100 g (4 oz) black treacle*
*100 g (4 oz) golden syrup*
*2 eggs, beaten*
*150 ml (5 fl oz) natural yoghurt*
*225 g (8 oz) wholemeal flour*
*1 teaspoon mixed spice*
*2 teaspoons ground ginger*
*¹/₂ teaspoon bicarbonate of soda*
*100 g (4 oz) preserved ginger, chopped*
*50 g (2 oz) mixed candied peel, chopped*
*50 g (2 oz) blanched almonds, chopped*

Grease a baking tin 18 cm (7 in) square.

Put the butter, sugar, treacle and syrup into a small pan over a low heat until the butter has melted and the sugar dissolved. Remove the pan from the heat and allow to cool. Using a wooden spoon, stir the beaten eggs and the yoghurt into the syrup mixture. Sift together the flour, spices and bicarbonate of soda into a large mixing bowl and gradually pour on the syrup and eggs, beating well with a wooden spoon. Stir in the chopped ginger, candied peel and almonds and mix well.

Pour the mixture into the prepared baking tin and bake at 150°C(300°F)/Gas 2 for 1½ hours. Leave to cool in the tin.

The gingerbread really does improve with keeping and so should be made at least a day in advance of serving.

*Serves 8–10*

## Bran Bread

A cross between bread and cake, this is a rich brown loaf with dried fruit and walnuts.

*75 g (3 oz) wholemeal flour*
*75 g (3 oz) self-raising flour*
*1 teaspoon bicarbonate of soda*
*25 g (1 oz) bran*
*½ tespoon mixed spice*
*¼ teaspoon salt*
*1 egg*
*4 tablespoons vegetable oil*
*100 g (4 oz) soft dark brown sugar*
*grated rind of 1 orange*
*150 ml (5 fl oz) natural yoghurt*
*50 g (2 oz) sultanas*
*50 g (2 oz) walnuts, chopped*

Grease a 1-kg (2-lb) loaf tin and line it with greased greaseproof paper.

In a large bowl, mix together the wholemeal and self-raising flours, the bicarbonate of soda, bran, mixed spice and salt. Beat together the egg, vegetable oil, sugar, orange rind and yoghurt and slowly add to the dry ingredients. Beat well, then add the sultanas and chopped walnuts.

Pour the mixture into the lined loaf tin and bake at 190°C(375°F)/Gas 5 for 1 hour, until the loaf is well risen. Cool in the tin for 5 minutes, then turn out on to a wire rack to cool. Serve sliced and buttered.

*Serves 8*

## Soda Bread

Yeast cookery is lovely, but there isn't always time. Soda bread, divine straight from the oven, is made in minutes.

*450 g (1 lb) flour*
*1 teaspoon salt*
*½ teaspoon bicarbonate of soda*
*25 g (1 oz) butter*
*150 ml (5 fl oz) natural yoghurt*
*150 ml (¼ pint) milk*

Sift the flour, salt and soda together into a bowl and rub in the butter. Beat the yoghurt and milk together and gradually pour on to the dry ingredients. Mix with a spatula to form a stiff dough. Knead the dough in the bowl, then shape it into a circle about 5 cm (2 ins) thick. With a knife mark the dough into four wedges. Put it on to a pre-heated, ungreased, baking tray and bake at 170°C(325°F)/Gas 3 for 25–30 minutes until the bread is well risen and firm.
*Serves 4–8*

## Honey Bread
Crisp, pancake-like bread that's crunchy and different.

*225 g (8 oz) wholemeal flour*
*1 teaspoon salt*
*1/2 teaspoon caraway seeds*
*50 g (2 oz) butter*
*1 tablespoon clear honey*
*225 ml (8 fl oz) natural yoghurt*

Stir the flour, salt and caraway seeds together in a bowl. Rub the butter in with the fingertips, then stir in the honey and yoghurt. Knead the dough lightly until it is smooth.

Divide the dough up into golf-ball-sized pieces and roll them out on a lightly-floured board until they are very thin, like pancakes.

Grease a griddle iron or heavy-based frying pan, heat it and then cook the dough circles a few at a time over a high heat. The bread will bubble on the surface and become crisp.

Serve with yoghurt cheese, lemon curd or honey.
*Makes 8–10*

## Corn Bread
It is said that there are as many recipes for corn bread as there are American housewives to bake it. This one, with a generous measure of yoghurt, has a marvellous sweet-and-sour flavour which makes it ideal not only at tea-time, but to serve with soups and savoury dishes. If you can't find the coarsely-ground corn meal use polenta, which is sold in most delicatessen shops. This more finely ground flour doesn't affect the flavour, but gives a closer texture.

*175 g (6 oz) corn meal* or *polenta*
*225 g (8 oz) flour*
*3 teaspoons baking powder*
*3/4 teaspoon salt*
*75 g (3 oz) sugar*
*225 ml (8 oz) natural yoghurt*
*60 ml (2 fl oz) milk*
*1 egg, well beaten*
*2 tablespoons margarine* or *lard, melted and cooled*

Grease a 20 by 20-cm (8 by 8-in) baking tin.

Put the corn meal in a bowl and sift in the flour, baking powder, salt and sugar. Or sift the polenta together with these dry ingredients. Add the yoghurt, milk, beaten egg and melted fat and mix well with a wooden spoon. Turn the mixture into the greased tin and bake at 220°C(425°F)/Gas 7 for 20 minutes. To enjoy the bread at its very best serve it hot with butter.

## High-rise Yoghurt Scones

Try using yoghurt instead of sour milk in scones. The taste is perfect and the appearance positively prize-winning.

*225 g (8 oz) flour*
*¹/₂ teaspoon salt*
*1¹/₂ teaspoons baking powder*
*25 g (1 oz) butter*
*150 ml (5 fl oz) natural yoghurt*

Sift together the flour, salt and baking powder and rub in the butter with the fingertips, until the mixture resembles fine breadcrumbs. Add the yoghurt and, using a palette knife, mix to a soft dough.

On a lightly-floured board, knead the dough until it is smooth, then roll out to a thickness of about 1 cm (¹/₂ in). Cut into rounds with a pastry cutter and place on a greased baking tray. Bake near the top of a pre-heated oven at 200°C(400°F)/Gas 6 for 12–15 minutes, until the scones are well risen and golden brown. Transfer them to a wire rack.

Serve the scones split and buttered, with a strongly-flavoured preserve such as elderberry jelly or bramble jam.
*Makes 10–12*

## Honey Scones

When it is strawberries-for-tea time, make these wonderfully light scones to serve with cream. Out of season, partner the scones with bramble or elderberry jelly.

*225 g (8 oz) self-raising flour*
*pinch salt*
*50 g (2 oz) butter*
*grated zest of ¹/₂ lemon*
*1 tablespoon clear honey*
*150 ml (5 fl oz) natural yoghurt*
*milk to glaze*

For filling
*150 ml (¹/₄ pint) double cream, lightly whipped*
*225 g (8 oz) strawberries, hulled and quartered*

Sift together the flour and salt in a mixing bowl and rub in the butter with the fingertips, until the mixture resembles fine breadcrumbs. Stir in the lemon zest. Mix together the honey and yoghurt and add to the flour mixture. Stir with a palette knife to form a soft dough.

Knead the dough lightly on a floured surface until smooth and roll out to a 1-cm (½-in) thickness. Cut into rounds with a fluted pastry cutter and place on a greased baking sheet. Brush with milk to glaze and bake near the top of the oven at 220°C(425°F)/Gas 7 for 12–15 minutes, until the scones are well risen and golden brown. Transfer them to a wire rack to cool.

Split the scones and fill with the whipped cream and strawberries.
*Makes 8–10*

## Wholemeal Scone Round
A filling of plain yoghurt cheese and honey, or the *pashka* cheese filling on page 46, brings out the flavour of this fruit scone round.

> 225 g (8 oz) wholemeal flour
> ½ teaspoon salt
> 1½ teaspoons baking powder
> 25 g (1 oz) butter
> 50 g (2 oz) sultanas
> 150 ml (5 fl oz) natural yoghurt

Mix the flour, salt and baking powder together in a bowl and rub in the butter with the fingertips. Stir in the sultanas and, using a palette knife, the yoghurt. Mix to a soft dough and knead lightly. Turn the dough out on to a lightly-floured board and roll to a thickness of almost 2 cm (¾ in). Shape into a circle and mark into eight sections. Place on a greased baking sheet. Bake near the top of the oven at 200°C(400°F)/Gas 6 for 12 minutes, until the scone is well risen.

Cut the scone into the 8 marked sections and split them. Spread with yoghurt cheese (page 5) on one half and honey on the other, then sandwich the 2 halves together. Or serve with the *pashka* filling.
*Serves 8*

## Treacle Scone
For a farmhouse-type tea, you could offer a selection of scones – plain, wholemeal, honey, treacle and savoury ones – and a selection of preserves and yoghurt cheese. It makes sense, because that way your baking makes the most of the high oven temperature.

> 225 g (8 oz) wholemeal flour
> ½ teaspoon bicarbonate of soda
> ½ teaspoon salt
> 2 teaspoons cream of tartar
> 25 g (1 oz) lard

*25 g (1 oz) soft light brown sugar*
*1 tablespoon black treacle*
*150 ml (5 fl oz) natural yoghurt*
*little milk*

Put the flour into a bowl and sift the soda, salt and cream of tartar on to it. Mix well, then rub in the lard with the fingertips. Stir in the sugar, treacle and yoghurt, using a palette knife. Add a very little milk if needed to make a soft dough.

Roll out the dough on a lightly-floured board to a thickness of about 1.5 cm (³/₄ in). Shape into a circle, then transfer to a baking sheet. Mark in 8 wedge-shaped sections and bake near the top of the oven at 230°C(450°F)/Gas 8 for 15–20 minutes, until the scone is well risen and golden brown.
*Serves 8*

## Grilled Scones
If you don't need to heat the oven for any other dish, it makes budget sense to grill a batch of scones to serve steaming hot, straight from the cooker. If you've been grilling toast or something savoury for tea, it makes more sense still.

*450 g (1 lb) self-raising flour*
*2 teaspoons baking powder*
*pinch salt*
*50 g (2 oz) butter or lard*
*2 eggs, beaten*
*180 ml (¹/₃ pint) milk*

*For filling*
*100 g (4 oz) yoghurt cheese (see page 5)*
*25g (1 oz) sultanas*
*15 g (¹/₂ oz) caster sugar (optional)*
*squeeze of lemon juice*

Sift together the flour, baking powder and salt into a bowl and rub in the fat. Stir in the beaten eggs and milk and mix to a soft dough. Knead the dough lightly to knock out the cracks and, on a lightly-floured board, roll out to a thickness of 1 cm (¹/₂ in). Using a small pastry cutter, cut into circles.

Line the grill pan with foil and turn the grill to the highest temperature. Put the scones on the grill pan and turn the heat down to moderate. Grill the scones for 10 minutes on each side, until they are well risen and medium brown.

Serve the scones straight from the grill, split and filled with the cheese and fruit mixture.

To make the filling, beat the yoghurt cheese in a bowl and stir in the sultanas and, if a sweet filling is required, the sugar. Add a few drops of lemon juice and mix well.
*Makes 16 scones*

## Girdle Cakes

Traditionally these cakes are cooked by dropping spoonfuls of the batter on to a heated griddle iron – griddle cakes is another name for them. A large, heavy-based frying pan, though perhaps less beautiful to look at, is just as effective.

*100 g (4 oz) flour*
*½ teaspoon bicarbonate of soda*
*½ teaspoon salt*
*25 g (1 oz) sugar*
*150 ml (5 fl oz) natural yoghurt*
*2 tablespoons milk*
*25 g (1 oz) butter, softened*
*1 egg*

Sift together the flour, soda, salt and sugar. Beat together the yoghurt, milk, softened butter and egg and fold in the dry ingredients. Stir to mix well, and add a little more milk if necessary to make a thick pouring batter.

Lightly grease a griddle or frying pan and heat it over a moderate to high heat. Drop tablespoons of the batter on to the heated surface and cook until the scones bubble and the undersides are brown. Flip the scones over with a spatula or fish slice and cook the other sides. Keep the cooked cakes warm in a dish covered by a teatowel while you cook the rest.

These griddle cakes are best if eaten warm. In any case, eat them the same day, unless they are to be stored in a freezer. They do not keep well in a tin. Serve them with butter and raspberry or loganberry jam.
*Makes about 15 cakes*


## Fruit Puffs

Light-as-air choux buns are a lovely luxury for tea, or good as a party dessert. These are filled with soft berry fruits, yoghurt cheese and honey.

*50 g (2 oz) butter*
*150 ml (¼ pint) water*
*pinch salt*
*65 g (2½ oz) flour, sifted*
*1 egg*

For filling
*225 g (8 oz) soft fruit – raspberries, strawberries* or *loganberries – hulled*
*150 g (5 oz) yoghurt cheese (see page 5)*
*1 tablespoon clear honey*
*icing sugar to decorate*

To make the pastry, put the butter, water and salt in a pan over a moderate heat until the butter has melted, then bring to the boil. Remove from the heat and beat in the sifted flour. Beat until smooth. Allow the mixture to cool a little, then beat in the egg. The pastry should form a ball and leave the sides of the pan clean.

Place small spoonfuls of the mixture on a lightly-greased baking tray and bake at 190°C(375°F)/Gas 5 for 20–30 minutes, until the pastry has puffed up and is cooked through.

Remove the puffs to a wire rack and immediately split them horizontally with a knife, leaving one side still attached. (It is important to allow the steam to escape as soon as the pastry is taken out of the oven.) When the puffs are cold, fill them with the cheese mixture.

To make the filling, halve or quarter the strawberries if they are large. Put the yoghurt cheese into a bowl and stir in the fruit and honey; add a little more honey if a sweeter mixture is preferred. Fill the buns, then dust them lightly with icing sugar shaken through a sieve.
*Makes 6–8 puffs*


## Hurry-up Cheesecake

Cheesecakes of all kind, from the traditional lattice, baked variety to this made-in-a-minute one, are immensely popular with all age groups. This one, flavoured with honey and orange, could be served both at tea-time and at an informal supper.

*75 g (3 oz) butter*
*175 g (6 oz) digestive biscuits, crushed*
*¹/₂ tablet orange jelly*
*150 ml (¹/₄ pint) water, boiling*
*175 g (6 oz) yoghurt cheese (see page 5)*
*2 tablespoons clear honey*
*1 orange*
*150 ml (5 fl oz) natural yoghurt, whipped*
*slices of orange or candied orange to decorate*

Melt the butter in a pan over a low heat and stir in the biscuit crumbs. Press the mixture into a 20-cm (8-in) flan ring on a baking tray, or a flan case with a removable base.

Cut the jelly tablet into cubes, put them in a small bowl and pour on the boiling water. Stir until the jelly dissolves.

Mix together the yoghurt cheese, honey, grated zest and strained juice of the orange and gradually pour on the jelly, stirring. Leave until the mixture is beginning to set, then whisk for a few seconds. Stir in the whipped yoghurt and pour into the biscuit case. Leave in the refrigerator or a cold place to set. Remove the flan ring, or remove the cheesecake from the flan case and put on to a serving plate. Decorate with orange slices.
*Serves 6*

## Almond Cheesecake

Crushed macaroons for the base give this honey and orange cheesecake mixture a very sophisticated standing.

75 g (3 oz) butter
225 g (8 oz) almond macaroons, crushed

For filling
225 g (8 oz) yoghurt cheese (see page 5)
150 ml (5 fl oz) natural yoghurt
2 tablespoons clear honey
grated zest of 1 orange
1 tablespoon blanched almonds, toasted and roughly chopped
slices of orange to decorate
few ratafia biscuit drops to decorate

Melt the butter in a small pan and stir in the crushed macaroons. Press into a 20-cm (8-in) flan ring on a baking tray, or a flan case with a removable base.

Beat the yoghurt cheese and yoghurt together in a bowl and mix with the honey, grated orange rind and chopped almonds. Pour into the chilled biscuit base and leave in the refrigerator or a cold place to set. Decorate with orange slices and tiny ratafia biscuits.
*Serves 6*

## Honey Cheesecake

Honey and banana, a lovely combination for tea-time.

75 g (3 oz) butter
175 g (6 oz) digestive biscuits, crushed

For filling
225 g (8 oz) yoghurt cheese (see page 5)
150 ml (5 fl oz) natural yoghurt
2 eggs
2 tablespoons clear honey
15 g (½ oz) powdered gelatine
2 tablespoons water
2 bananas, sliced slantwise
1 tablespoon lemon juice

Grease a 20-cm (8-in) flan ring on a baking tray or a flan case with removable base.

Melt the butter in a small pan, stir in the crushed biscuits and press into the flan ring or flan case. Set aside to cool while making the filling.

To make the filling, beat together the yoghurt cheese, yoghurt, eggs and honey. Sprinkle the gelatine on to the water in a small bowl. Stand in a bowl of hot water and stir until the gelatine has dissolved. Allow to cool, then mix thoroughly

into the cheese mixture. Pour the filling into the biscuit base and chill before serving. Decorate with sliced banana dipped in lemon juice.
*Serves 6*

## Belgian Cheese Tart
It's simplicity itself to make, and deliciously smooth. Serve it as a dessert, too, with stewed blackcurrants or loganberries.

*215-g (7-oz) packet frozen puff pastry*
*225 g (8 oz) yoghurt cheese (see page 5)*
*2 eggs, beaten*
*150 ml (¼ pint) double cream*
*½ lemon*
*40 g (1½ oz) caster sugar*
*1 tablespoon currants*

Roll out the pastry on a lightly-floured board and lift it to line a 20-cm (8-in) flan ring on a baking tray. Take care not to stretch the pastry, or it will shrink in cooking. Put it in the refrigerator or a cold place to chill for 30 minutes. Line the pastry case with foil and fill with 'baking beans'. Bake blind at 220°C(425°F)/ Gas 7 for 15 minutes, remove foil and beans and bake for a further 5 minutes to dry the pastry case.

Put the yoghurt cheese into a bowl and gradually beat in the eggs, a little at a time. Beat until the mixture is smooth, then stir in the cream, grated rind and strained juice of the lemon, the sugar and currants. Do not beat the mixture at this stage.

Turn the filling into the flan case and bake at 180°C(350°F)/Gas 4 for 25 minutes, until the filling is set firm. Allow to cool in the flan ring. Turn out on to a serving plate and serve cold.
*Serves 6*

## Tomato and Onion Teabread
It's good to have a repertoire of savoury teabreads to give the phrase 'bread and butter' an air of mystery occasionally.

*225 g (8 oz) self-raising flour*
*½ teaspoon salt*
*¼ teaspoon mixed dried herbs*
*25 g (1 oz) margarine*
*1 tablespoon fresh chopped parsley*
*1 small onion, skinned and grated*
*2 medium-sized tomatoes, peeled*
*1 egg*
*150 ml (5 fl oz) natural yoghurt*
*little milk*

Grease a 450-g (1-lb) loaf tin.

Sift together the flour, salt and dried herbs into a bowl and rub in the margarine until the mixture resembles fine breadcrumbs. Stir in the chopped parsley and grated onion. Halve the peeled tomatoes, remove the seeds and chop the flesh. Beat the egg and yoghurt together and add to the flour mixture with the tomato flesh. Add 1 tablespoon of milk if the mixture is too stiff.

Turn into the prepared loaf tin and bake at 190°C(375°F)/Gas 5 for 40–50 minutes, until the loaf is well risen and golden brown.

Serve, sliced and buttered, with cheese and salad for high tea.
*Serves 8*


## Peanut Butter Teabread

Crunchy peanuts on top of a savoury teabread made rich and moist with peanut butter – it can't fail with the children!

*225 g (8 oz) self-raising flour*
*1/2 teaspoon salt*
*pinch pepper*
*1/4 teaspoon garlic powder*
*25 g (1 oz) margarine*
*2 stalks celery, washed and finely chopped*
*75 g (3 oz) crunchy peanut butter*
*1 egg*
*150 ml (5 fl oz) natural yoghurt*
*little milk*
*1 tablespoon salted peanuts*

Grease a 450-g (1-lb) loaf tin.

Sift together the flour, salt, pepper and garlic powder into a bowl. Rub in the margarine until the mixture resembles fine breadcrumbs, then stir in the celery and peanut butter. Beat together the egg and yoghurt and add to the mixture with 1 tablespoon of milk if it is too stiff.

Turn the mixture into the loaf tin, spread it evenly and sprinkle with the salted peanuts. Bake at 190°C(375°F)/Gas 5 for 40–50 minutes, until well risen and golden brown.

Serve sliced with butter or thinly-spread peanut butter.
*Serves 8*


## Bacon Scones

For high tea, or for people whose tastes lean towards savoury things, these scones are unusual and delicious. To give them the extra advantage of being economical, try to buy bacon trimmings from your grocer – so much cheaper than rashers.

*100 g (4 oz) bacon, de-rinded and chopped*
*225 g (8 oz) wholemeal flour*
*50 g (2 oz) margarine*
*1 teaspoon dried mixed herbs*
*100 g (4 oz) Cheddar cheese, grated*
*¼ teaspoon celery salt*
*salt*
*freshly-ground black pepper*
*pinch cayenne pepper*
*120 ml (4 fl oz) natural yoghurt*

In a small non-stick frying pan, fry the chopped bacon over a low heat until the fat runs. Remove the bacon from the pan and set aside to cool.

Put the flour into a bowl and rub in the margarine with the fingertips, until the mixture resembles fine breadcrumbs. Stir in the bacon, herbs and cheese and season with celery salt, salt and pepper. Stir in the yoghurt, using a palette knife. Knead the dough in the bowl until it is smooth.

Turn the dough out on to a lightly-floured board and roll to a rectangle about 2 cm (¾ in) thick. With a knife trim the edges and mark the dough into squares. Transfer the dough to a greased baking sheet and bake at 220°C(425°F)/Gas 7 for 20–25 minutes, until the scone is well risen and golden brown.

Ideally, serve hot with butter. The scone is also a good accompaniment to cold meats.
*Serves 8*


**Cheese Muffins**
Unfortunately, the muffin man no longer rings his bell, inviting us to rush out into the street and buy hot muffins from the tray on his head. But if you ring a bell when these cheese ones are ready, people are sure to come running!

*350 g (12 oz) self-raising flour*
*2 teaspoons baking powder*
*pinch salt*
*100 g (4 oz) Wensleydale cheese, finely grated*
*1 large egg, beaten*
*1 tablespoon natural yoghurt*
*milk to glaze*

Sift together the flour, baking powder and salt and stir in the cheese. Add the beaten egg and the yoghurt to make a soft but not sticky dough. Knead the dough well to make it smooth, then roll out on a lightly-floured board to about 2 cm (¾ in) thick. Using a pastry cutter, cut the dough into rounds. Brush the tops with milk and place on a lightly-greased baking tray. Cook near the top of the oven, pre-heated to 230°C(450°F)/Gas 8, until the muffins are well risen and golden brown.

Serve the muffins hot, cut in halves and buttered, or cold, spread with yoghurt cheese.

*Makes 16–18 muffins*

# TEA-TIME SANDWICHES

One of the measures of elegance in society houses used to be the thinness of the bread cut for tea-time sandwiches. Wafer-thin sandwiches of paper-thin cucumber were the height of gentility at bridge or tennis parties – and still seem luxurious, even today.

But sandwiches have grown up in the intervening years. They can be filled with anything from a sparing scrape of anchovy paste to a fried egg and a rasher of bacon, and the bread can range from factory-sliced to a whole French loaf split asunder and packed with colourful layers.

Here are a few ideas for sweet and savoury sandwich fillings, not only for tea-time – for working lunches, picnics, lunch or supper buffet parties and late-night snacks, some even for scones and sponge sandwich cakes. They have one thing in common, of course – a measure of yoghurt.

## Sandwich Kebabs

Mini cubed sandwiches threaded on to cocktail sticks are much more fun than the same sandwiches piled on a plate. Make them from a variety of breads – white, wholemeal, rye, caraway and so on – and with a choice of spreads (see ideas below).

Make the sandwiches in the usual way, some white and some brown, and with different fillings. Wrap the sandwiches tightly in foil and refrigerate for at least 2 hours. To serve, cut off the crusts and cut each sandwich into sixteen mini squares. Thread the sandwiches, alternating white and brown breads, on to cocktail sticks. Decorate the end of each stick with a cube of pineapple, a cocktail onion, a stuffed green olive, a cube of cheese or a radish. Push the cocktail sticks into a large potato or a grapefruit to serve.

## Kipper Spread

*175-g (6-oz) packet frozen kipper fillets*
*juice of 1/2 lemon*
*50 g (2 oz) yoghurt cheese (see page 5)*
*salt*
*freshly-ground black pepper*
*1 teaspoon fresh chopped chives*

Poach the kipper fillets in a little water for 6–8 minutes until cooked, then drain and leave to cool. Skin and flake the fish, then pound together with the lemon juice and yoghurt cheese until smooth. Season with salt and pepper and stir in the chopped chives.
*Makes enough for 1 small loaf*

### Liptauer Cheese

> *100 g (4 oz) yoghurt cheese (see page 5)*
> *50 g (2 oz) butter, softened*
> *1/4 teaspoon made mustard*
> *4 anchovy fillets, pounded*
> *4 small gherkins, finely chopped*
> *salt*
> *freshly-ground black pepper*
> *pinch cayenne pepper*

Beat together the yoghurt cheese and butter and stir in the remaining ingredients. Beat to blend well.
*Makes enough for 1 small loaf*

### Crab and Yoghurt Cheese

> *100 g (4 oz) yoghurt cheese (see page 5)*
> *50 g (2 oz) butter, softened*
> *50-g (2-oz) can dressed crab*
> *salt*
> *pinch cayenne pepper*

Beat together the yoghurt cheese and butter, stir in the dressed crab and season well.
*Makes enough for 1 small loaf*

### Devilled Ham

> *100 g (4 oz) ham, finely chopped or minced*
> *50 g (2 oz) butter, softened*
> *50 g (2 oz) yoghurt cheese (see page 5)*
> *2 teaspoons Worcestershire sauce*
> *1/4 teaspoon made mustard*
> *salt*
> *freshly-ground black pepper*

Cream together the ham, butter and yoghurt cheese and blend in the other ingredients until the mixture is smooth.
*Makes enough for 1 small loaf*

## Banana Spread

*3 bananas, mashed*
*100 g (4 oz) yoghurt cheese (see page 5)*
*25 g (1 oz) walnuts, finely chopped*
*1 tablespoon chocolate spread*

Blend all the ingredients together until smooth. The chocolate spread will take care of any darkening of the bananas under refrigeration.
*Makes enough for 1 small loaf*


## Date Spread

*75 g (3 oz) stoned dates, finely chopped*
*100 g (4 oz) yoghurt cheese (see page 5)*
*1 teaspoon lemon juice*
*pinch nutmeg*

Beat the dates into the yoghurt cheese, add the lemon juice and nutmeg and beat until the mixture is smooth.
*Makes enough for 1 small loaf*


## Apricot Spread

*90 ml (3 fl oz) thick apricot or other fruit purée*
*125 g (5 oz) yoghurt cheese (see page 5)*
*25 g (1 oz) blanched almonds, finely chopped*
*2 drops almond essence*

Beat the fruit purée into the yoghurt cheese until well blended, then beat in the chopped nuts and almond essence.
*Makes enough for 1 small loaf*


## Peanut Crunch

*100 g (4 oz) yoghurt cheese (see page 5)*
*2 tablespoons crunchy peanut butter*
*40 g (1¹/₂ oz) salted peanuts, milled*
*1 teaspoon lemon juice*

Beat together the yoghurt cheese and peanut butter until smooth. Grind the peanuts in a food mill or blender and beat into the cheese mixture with the lemon juice.
*Makes enough for 1 small loaf*

## Herby Yoghurt Sandwiches

*50 g (2 oz) Cheddar cheese, grated*
*2 tablespoons natural yoghurt*
*1 tablespoon fresh chopped chives*
*salt*
*freshly-ground black pepper*
*4 thin slices brown bread, cut from large loaf*

Combine the grated cheese, yoghurt and chives in a small bowl. Season with salt and pepper and spread on two of the bread slices. Cover with the other slices and cut into fingers. Serve with crisp sticks of raw celery, carrot or cauliflower.

As a variation, substitute 1 tablespoon finely-chopped gherkin or capers. These slightly 'sour' flavours combine particularly well with yoghurt.
*Makes 8 finger sandwiches*

## Olive Pinwheels

Stuffed olives, with their bright juxtaposition of red and green, can replace asparagus in rolled sandwiches that look irresistible.

*1 large white sandwich tin loaf*
*butter, softened*
*175 g (6 oz) yoghurt cheese (see page 5)*
*about 24 stuffed green olives*

Cut the crusts from the bread and cut the loaf lengthwise into six slices. Butter each slice very sparingly, then spread with yoghurt cheese. Place four olives in a row at one end of a slice of bread and roll up, starting at the end with the olives, like a Swiss roll. Roll tightly in greaseproof paper and leave in the refrigerator or a cold place for at least 12 hours, then unwrap and slice into pinwheels – you should have 6 rolls, each sliced into 6 pinwheels.

These sandwiches freeze well. Freeze them before slicing into wheels, then thaw in the refrigerator for 2 hours before cutting up.
*Makes 36 pinwheels*

CHAPTER FIVE

# *Off to a Good Start*

The first course of a meal should never be the poor relation. Quite naturally, the main course is the first item to be decided when planning the menu. That's as it should be, since it will almost certainly represent the greatest expense, and should be chosen according to what's in season, or specially recommended at the time by the butcher, fishmonger or grocer.

But the first course will set the mood for the meal, before the smells wafting from the kitchen reveal the secret of the main dish. Consider the opening course in the same way as the entrance hall of a house: people have to pass through it before they can know how much trouble you have taken with what's to follow.

So here's to good and lasting first impressions! Most of the recipes in this chapter can be made a day in advance of a dinner party and left ready and waiting, or at the very most just need heating at the last moment. They range from chilled or heart-warming soups to vegetable dishes and salads, with a small section at the end of hors d'oeuvres to be served as cocktail savouries or as a first course with drinks, before guests sit down to the meal. Some of them such as Jellied Tomato Soup and Shropshire Onions, demonstrate the important part yoghurt has to play as a dressing or sauce, harmonizing with stronger flavours. If your choice is a hot soup, take care to leave it over a low heat without allowing it to boil, especially after the addition of yoghurt or cream; otherwise the texture will be spoiled.

Choose your opening course according to the richness or complexity of the main dish and pudding. And whatever you do, don't flatter – and dismay – your guests with a surfeit of creaminess. If the main dish has a creamy sauce, choose, perhaps, Spinach and Leek Salad or Omelette Ribbons to start. With a roast or grill for the main course, feel free to range among the thickened soups or cheesy starters.

Choose your first course, prepare it and then relax so that you, too, make a good first impression on the evening!

## Chilled Lemon Soup
A busy cook's standby, a refreshing soup that's made in moments.

> *0.5-kg (19-oz) can tomato juice*
> *600 ml (20 fl oz) natural yoghurt, chilled*
> *1/2 medium-sized cucumber, cut into 0.5-cm (1/4-in) cubes*
> *2 spring onions, trimmed and chopped*
> *grated zest and juice of 1 lemon*
> *salt*
> *freshly-ground black pepper*
> *cayenne pepper*
> *1 tablespoon fresh chopped chives to garnish*
> *extra cucumber and lemon slices to garnish*

In a large bowl, whisk together the tomato juice and yoghurt. Stir in the chopped cucumber and onion and the zest and juice of the lemon. Season well with salt and pepper and add a pinch of cayenne pepper to give the soup 'sparkle'. Store until needed in the refrigerator, in a covered bowl. Serve in chilled bowls, garnished with chopped chives and very thin slices of cucumber and lemon.
*Serves 4–6*

## Raspberry Soup
One of the most luxurious ways to serve soft fruit, if you have a generous crop, is as a chilled soup. This recipe calls for only about 450 g (1 lb) raspberries and will probably win more compliments than if they were served in any other way.

> *1 small wineglass red wine*
> *3 tablespoons clear honey*
> *2 tablespoons water*
> *300 ml (1/2 pint) raspberry purée*
> *150 ml (5 fl oz) natural yoghurt, chilled*
> *ground nutmeg*

Put the wine, honey and water into a small pan over a low heat until the honey has dissolved. While the mixture is still warm, stir in the raspberry purée and blend well. Leave the mixture to cool, then stir in the yoghurt, reserving a little to decorate. Chill the soup in the refrigerator or a cold place.

Serve the soup in chilled bowls, each portion swirled with a teaspoon of yoghurt sprinkled with nutmeg. Serve with unsweetened biscuits.
*Serves 4*

## Chilled Mushroom Soup

You could plan to serve this soup cold on a hot day. If the weather turns nasty, simply heat it again. It will be just as delicious, and a good deal more appropriate.

*900 ml (1 1/2 pints) well-flavoured chicken stock*
*225 g (8 oz) mushrooms, washed and roughly chopped (reserve a few*
  *slices to garnish)*
*salt*
*freshly-ground black pepper*
*1 tablespoon arrowroot*
*300 ml (1/2 pint) milk*
*150 ml (5 fl oz) natural yoghurt, chilled*
*1 tablespoon fresh chopped mint*

Skim the chicken stock of any fat, which would ruin a chilled soup. Put it into a large saucepan, add the chopped mushrooms and season with salt and pepper. Cover, bring to the boil and simmer for 10 minutes. Liquidize or strain through a sieve and return to the pan.

In a small bowl, blend the arrowroot with a little of the milk to make a smooth, thin paste. Pour into the soup with the remaining milk and bring just to the boil. Taste for seasoning and add more if necessary.

Pour the soup into a container, leave to cool then put in the refrigerator to chill. Pour into a tureen.

Whip the yoghurt and swirl into the chilled soup. Scatter the chopped mint on top to garnish and enhance the cool effect.

*Serves 6*

## Iced Watercress Soup

This soup is best made a day in advance, so that the watercress flavour can fully assert itself.

*600 ml (1 pint) chicken stock, skimmed of fat*
*450 g (1 lb) potatoes, peeled*
*450 g (1 lb) leeks, washed and trimmed*
*1 bunch watercress, washed, picked over and chopped (reserve a few*
  *sprigs to garnish)*
*75 g (3 oz) butter*
*salt*
*freshly-ground black pepper*
*300 ml (10 fl oz) natural yoghurt, chilled*
*6 ice-cubes, to serve*

Put the chicken stock in a saucepan and boil the potatoes and leeks in it until they are tender. Liquidize the cooked vegetables, together with the watercress. Without a liquidizer, rub the cooked vegetables through a sieve, chop the watercress finely and add, with the vegetable purée, to the stock. Add the butter, to melt in the hot soup.

Pour the soup into a container, cover, leave to cool and store overnight in the refrigerator. Season well with salt and pepper. Beat in the yoghurt and serve in individual ice-cold bowls, garnished with an ice-cube and a sprig of watercress.
*Serves 6*


## Jellied Tomato Soup

An elegant jellied soup to serve for a dinner party. The cool yoghurt topping contrasts well with the richness of the tomato base.

*10-cm (4-in) length cucumber, diced*
*450 g (1 lb) tomatoes, cut in quarters*
*15 g (¹/₂ oz) sugar*
*¹/₄ teaspoon salt*
*few grinds of black pepper*
*450 ml (³/₄ pint) water*
*15 g (¹/₂ oz) powdered gelatine*
*3 tablespoons water, warm*
*3 teaspoons vinegar*
*4 tablespoons natural yoghurt, chilled*
*1 tablespoon fresh chopped parsley, to garnish*

Put the cucumber, tomatoes, sugar and seasoning in a pan with 450 ml (³/₄ pint) water. Cover, bring to the boil and simmer for 30 minutes. Strain through a fine sieve to remove seeds and tomato skin.

Sprinkle the gelatine on to 3 tablespoons warm water in a cup or small bowl, and stir to dissolve. Pour the gelatine liquid into the strained tomato liquid, add the vinegar and taste for seasoning. Add more salt and pepper if needed. Leave the soup to cool, then put in the refrigerator to set.

When it has set firm, break up the jelly with a fork and divide between serving bowls. Top each one with 1 tablespoon chilled yoghurt and garnish with chopped parsley.
*Serves 4*


## Almond Soup

This soup was a nineteenth-century favourite. It's rather special these days, the price of almonds being what it is, but a good start to a dinner party.

*1 litre (2 pints) chicken stock*
*1 stalk celery, washed and chopped*
*1 bouquet garni*
*2 bayleaves*

*1 blade mace*
*salt*
*freshly-ground white pepper*
*225 g (8 oz) almonds, blanched*
*1 small glass medium sherry*
*120 ml (4 fl oz) natural yoghurt*

Put the stock into a large saucepan, add the celery, herbs and mace and season lightly with salt and white pepper. Bring slowly to the boil and simmer for 25–30 minutes, skimming once or twice. Remove from the heat and then strain. Reserving a few almonds to garnish, grind the remaining nuts in a blender, or crush them in a polythene bag with a rolling pin. Pour the stock into a flameproof casserole, add the almonds and sherry and bring just to boiling point again. Simmer gently for 20 minutes. Stir in the yoghurt and reheat without boiling. Serve hot, garnished with the reserved almonds cut into thin slivers and lightly toasted.
*Serves 4*

## Carrot Soup
The colour of russety, autumn leaves, this is one of the most attractive of all soups. Use the largest carrots – in the creamy broth they will taste like young spring vegetables.

*675 g (1 ½ lb) carrots, peeled or scraped and sliced*
*½ teaspoon sugar*
*50 g (2 oz) butter*
*25 g (1 oz) flour*
*1 litre (2 pints) chicken stock, warm*
*salt*
*freshly-ground black pepper*
*2 egg yolks*
*150 ml (5 fl oz) natural yoghurt*

Reserving one of the smallest carrots to garnish, cook the remainder in boiling, salted water until tender – about 15 minutes. Put in a blender or rub through a sieve. Add the sugar to the purée. Melt the butter in a large flameproof casserole, add the flour and stir to make a roux. When it forms a ball, gradually add a little of the stock, stirring until it is the consistency of a thin sauce. Add the carrot purée, stirring well, then the remainder of the stock, still stirring. Season well with salt and pepper. Beat the egg yolks in a small bowl, beat in the yoghurt and gradually add a little of the warm soup. Add the egg mixture to the pan and heat without boiling. Slice the reserved raw carrot into wafer-thin rings (using a mandolin if you have one) and float them on the soup to garnish.
*Serves 4*

## Winter Garden Soup

You can vary the vegetables according to what you have in the garden, or which ones are cheap in the shops. This soup freezes well; in that case add the egg yolk and yoghurt on reheating.

*25 g (1·oz) butter*
*1 small onion, skinned and chopped*
*1 leek, washed, trimmed and chopped*
*2 stalks celery, washed and chopped*
*2 large carrots, washed or scrubbed, trimmed and chopped*
*1 medium-sized potato, peeled and chopped*
*2 bunches watercress, washed and picked over*
*1 tablespoon fresh chopped parsley*
*450 ml (³/₄ pint) chicken stock*
*salt*
*freshly-ground black pepper*
*150 ml (5 fl oz) natural yoghurt*
*1 egg yolk*

Melt the butter in a large pan and fry the chopped onion and leek over a moderate heat until soft but not coloured. Add the celery, carrots and potato and stir. Reserving four sprigs for garnish, chop the watercress and add to the pan with the parsley. Pour on the chicken stock, season with salt and pepper, stir well and cover. Bring to the boil and simmer for 15 minutes, until the vegetables are tender.

If you prefer a smooth, creamy soup, rub the soup through a sieve or liquidize. Otherwise it will be clear and light, and full of crisp, tender vegetables. Either way, beat all but four teaspoons of the yoghurt into the egg yolk and stir into the soup to reheat. Do not allow to boil. Serve garnished with the reserved yoghurt and sprigs of watercress.
*Serves 4*


## Potato and Bacon Soup

With bacon and paprika pepper, this potato soup has a little more 'bite' than most. It's good on a cold day.

*40 g (1¹/₂ oz) butter*
*1 small onion, skinned and chopped*
*4 rashers streaky bacon, without rind, chopped*
*1 tablespoon fresh chopped parsley*
*675 g (1¹/₂ lb) potatoes, peeled and cubed*
*40 g (1¹/₂ oz) flour*
*1 teaspoon paprika pepper*

*1 litre (2 pints) chicken stock*
*salt*
*150 ml (5 fl oz) natural yoghurt*
*1 tablespoon fresh chopped chives*

Melt the butter in a large pan, add the chopped onion and bacon and fry over a moderate heat for 3–4 minutes, until the bacon fat begins to run. Stir in the parsley and potatoes and cook for a further 2 minutes. Add the flour and paprika pepper, stir well, then gradually pour on the chicken stock, stirring. Add the salt, cover the pan, bring to the boil and simmer for 15 minutes, or until the potatoes are cooked.

Put the soup in a liquidizer; or push through a coarse sieve, retrieving the bacon pieces and returning them to the creamed soup. Stir in the yoghurt and reheat the soup, without boiling. Garnish with the chopped chives.
*Serves 6–8*

## Italian Tomato Soup
An all-the-year round soup made with canned tomatoes. You can, of course, use fresh ones when they are cheap and plentiful.

*25 g (1 oz) butter*
*1 stalk celery, washed and chopped*
*1 small onion, skinned and chopped*
*1 clove garlic, skinned and finely chopped*
*1 large carrot, peeled or scrubbed and chopped*
*400-g (15-oz) can tomatoes*
*grated zest and juice of 1 orange*
*450 ml (3/4 pint) chicken stock*
*1/2 teaspoon dried basil or oregano*
*1 teaspoon English mustard powder*
*2 tablespoons cornflour*
*salt*
*freshly-ground black pepper*
*120 ml (4 fl oz) natural yoghurt*
*pinch cayenne pepper*

Melt the butter in a large saucepan and fry the chopped celery, onion, garlic and carrot over a moderate heat for 3–4 minutes. Add the tomatoes, together with their liquid, the orange zest and juice, chicken stock and the dried herb. Cover, bring to the boil and simmer for 30 minutes.

Sieve the soup, or liquidize and then strain. Put the mustard and cornflour in a small bowl, stir in a little of the soup to make a smooth, thin paste, then pour into the soup. Season well with salt and pepper, cover and bring to the boil, stirring so that the soup thickens smoothly.

Pour the soup into a warmed tureen and swirl the yoghurt on top. Garnish the yoghurt with a fine sprinkling of cayenne pepper.
*Serves 6*

## Spinach and Leek Salad
An unusual combination of fresh vegetables, lightly tossed in a chilled dressing, makes a refreshing change.

*450 g (1 lb) spinach, washed and chopped*
*450 g (1 lb) leeks, washed, trimmed and chopped*
*2 bunches watercress, washed and picked over*

For dressing
*1 teaspoon Dijon mustard*
*1 teaspoon lemon juice*
*salt*
*freshly-ground black pepper*
*pinch cayenne pepper*
*150 ml (5 fl oz) natural yoghurt, chilled*

Blanch the spinach in boiling, salted water for about ½ minute, drain and plunge into a bowl of cold water. Blanch the leeks in a separate pan of boiling, salted water for 2–3 minutes, drain and refresh in cold water. Cut the watercress into neat sprigs.

When the vegetables are cold, drain them well, patting dry with kitchen paper, and mix the spinach, leeks and watercress together in a large salad bowl.

To make the dressing, blend the seasonings with the yoghurt and pour over the vegetables. Lightly toss them in the dressing, and serve with crusty French bread.
*Serves 4–6*

## Shropshire Onions
Practically all vegetables can be served individually, as an appetizing first course. Onions often get overlooked. I can't think why.

*900 g (2 lb) pickling-sized onions*
*1-litre (1³/₄-pint) bottle dry cider*
*100 g (4 oz) raisins*
*50 g (2 oz) soft dark brown sugar*
*pinch nutmeg*
*natural yoghurt, chilled*

Put the onions in a saucepan, cover with cold water and bring to the boil. In another pan, bring the cider to the boil and reduce to a quarter of the volume over a medium-to-high heat.

72

Drain the onions and skin them. Arrange them in the dish and sprinkle with the raisins. Stir the sugar into the reduced cider and pour over the onions. Cook in the oven at 180°C(350°F)/Gas 4 for 15 minutes, until the onions are tender. Remove them from the oven and allow to cool, then put in the refrigerator or a cold place to chill. Serve very cold, sprinkled with a pinch of nutmeg and with chilled yoghurt separately.
*Serves 4*


## Stuffed Avocado Pears

Avocado pears are delicious with a simple vinaigrette dressing; a little more substantial with this smooth blend of flavours.

*4 tablespoons natural yoghurt*
*25 g (1 oz) stuffed green olives, sliced*
*25 g (1 oz) small gherkins, chopped*
*1 teaspoon fresh chopped chives*
*salt*
*freshly-ground black pepper*
*2 avocado pears*

Put the yoghurt into a small bowl and stir in the olives, gherkins and chives. Season well with salt and pepper. Just before serving, cut the avocado pears in half, remove the stones and spoon in the dressing.
*Serves 4*


## Snow Pears

Crisp, home-grown pears are delicious filled with soft creamy cheese and walnuts. Another dish that's ready in minutes.

*225 g (8 oz) yoghurt cheese (see page 5)*
*25 g (1 oz) walnuts, chopped (reserve 4 halves to garnish)*
*1 dessert apple, peeled, cored and chopped*
*salt*
*freshly-ground black pepper*
*4 large, ripe dessert pears*
*juice of 1/2 lemon*

To serve
*lettuce or spinach leaves, washed*
*1 green pepper, trimmed and cut into strips*
*2 tomatoes, cut in wedges*

In a bowl, mix together the yoghurt cheese, walnuts and chopped apple and lightly season with salt and pepper. Cut the pears in half lengthwise and, using a stainless steel knife, remove the core. Dip the outsides of the fruit in lemon juice to retain the colour.

Pile the cheese mixture on to the pears and serve them on a bed of fresh young lettuce or spinach leaves, garnished with colourful vegetables or fruit such as green peppers and tomatoes, red peppers and unpeeled apples.
*Serves 4 or 8*


## Salad Basket

It's worth taking a little time and trouble to prepare the melon basket attractively. It makes all the difference to the appearance of the dish.

> *1 large melon*
> *2 oranges*
> *2 grapefruit*
> *225 g (8 oz) yoghurt cheese (see page 5)*
> *50 g (2 oz) mixed nuts, chopped*
>
> For dressing
> *juice of ¹/₂ lemon*
> *juice of 2 small oranges*
> *1 teaspoon grated orange rind*
> *1 tablespoon clear honey*
> *1 teaspoon fresh chopped mint*
> *4 sprigs mint to decorate*
> *few cocktail cherries to decorate basket (optional)*

To prepare the melon basket, cut across the middle of the fruit from each side, leaving about 3.5 cm (1¹/₂ ins) uncut in the middle at either end. These ends will form the base of the handle. Then, extending the line of the handle across the top of the melon, slice down to the middle on either side of it. Remove these 2 large melon wedges. Scoop out the seeds and discard. Scoop out the flesh from the 2 wedges and the main basket section and dice it. Using a sharp pair of kitchen scissors, cut all round the sides of the basket in V shapes.

Peel the oranges and grapefruit and separate into segments. Mix the fruit with the yoghurt cheese and nuts.

For the dressing, mix together the lemon and orange juice, the orange rind, honey and chopped mint. Just before serving, toss the fruit and cheese mixture in the dressing and spoon into the melon basket. Decorate with the sprigs of mint.

You can decorate one side of the basket handle with a bunch of cocktail cherries. Stick them in place by piercing them with a short length of cocktail stick pushed through the melon handle.
*Serves 4*

## Tomato Boats

When the main dish is high on calories and effort, it makes sense to make light of the opening course.

*4 very large, ripe tomatoes*
*1 stalk celery, washed and finely chopped*
*1 spring onion, trimmed and chopped*
*1 eating apple, peeled, cored and chopped*
*8–10 capers*
*175 g (6 oz) yoghurt cheese (see page 5)*
*salt*
*freshly-ground black pepper*

*To serve*
*lettuce leaves, washed*
*1 lemon, cut in quarters*

Cut the tops off the tomatoes and scoop out the seeds and some of the flesh, leaving firm 'walls'. Turn them upside-down to drain. Stir the chopped celery, onion, apple and the capers into the yoghurt cheese and season with a little salt and plenty of pepper. Spoon into the tomato shells and replace the lids at a rakish angle.

Serve the tomatoes on a bed of lettuce leaves garnished with lemon wedges.
*Serves 4*


## Cheese Pâté

Often one has a few small pieces of cheese in the refrigerator, not quite up to being presented afresh on the cheeseboard. Here's a good way of combining these and other flavours. Try blending Cheddar and Brie (however dry) and Wensleydale and Gouda.

*75 g (3 oz) Cheshire cheese, finely grated*
*75 g (3 oz) Stilton cheese, finely grated*
*175 g (6 oz) yoghurt cheese (see page 5)*
*1 tablespoon medium sherry*
*1 teaspoon Dijon mustard*
*2 teaspoons fresh, finely-chopped chives*
*salt*
*freshly-ground black pepper*
*raw vegetables to serve (see method)*

In a bowl, beat together the grated Cheshire and Stilton and the yoghurt cheese. Beat in the sherry, mustard and chopped chives, taste for seasoning and add salt and pepper. Either press into a pâté dish or shape into a block or a circle and wrap in foil. Chill in the refrigerator or a cold place for at least 1 hour before serving.

To serve, place the dish or the cheese on a large serving plate and surround by a selection of crisp, raw salad vegetables, such as sliced mushrooms, carrots, celery, cucumber or tomatoes.
*Serves 6*


## Watercress Cheese

This is a kind of potted cheese, well flavoured with watercress. Serve it as a pâté, with hot, buttered toast. Or as a cocktail savoury, spread on crisp little biscuits.

*225 g (8 oz) yoghurt cheese (see page 5)*
*75 g (3 oz) Cheddar cheese, finely grated*
*3 tablespoons double cream*
*2 bunches watercress, washed, picked over and chopped*
*1 medium-sized onion, skinned and finely chopped*
*50 g (2 oz) walnuts, chopped*
*salt*
*freshly-ground black pepper*
*pinch cayenne pepper*

In a bowl, mix together the yoghurt and grated cheese and beat in the double cream. Stir in the chopped watercress, onion and walnuts and season well with salt and pepper. Press the cheese mixture into small cocotte dishes, cover with foil and chill in the refrigerator or a cold place. Serve with hot, buttered toast.
*Serves 4–6*


## Kipper Pâté

*2 215-g (7½-oz) packets kipper fillets*
*50 g (2 oz) butter, softened*
*50 g (2 oz) yoghurt cheese (see page 5)*
*60 ml (2 fl oz) natural yoghurt*
*juice of 1 lemon*
*1 tablespoon fresh chopped chives*
*freshly-ground black pepper*
*lemon slices to garnish*

Remove the skin and bones from the kipper fillets. There is no need to cook them. Pound the fish in a bowl and beat in the softened butter, yoghurt cheese and yoghurt. Add the lemon juice and chopped chives and season well with black pepper.

Press the pâté into a small fish-shaped mould if available. Or shape it into a roll and wrap it in foil. Chill and cut into rounds. Serve garnished with lemon slices, with hot, buttered toast.
*Serves 4–6*

## Buckling with Horseradish Sauce

There are several types of smoked fish available now. And they all make delicious first courses or light meals in a hurry.

*2 buckling, skinned and divided into fillets*
*15-cm (6-in) length cucumber, finely sliced*
*1 lemon, quartered, to serve*

For dressing
*3 teaspoons horseradish sauce*
*150 ml (5 fl oz) natural yoghurt, chilled*
*1 teaspoon lemon juice*
*1 tablespoon fresh chopped parsley*
*salt*
*freshly-ground black pepper*
*pinch cayenne pepper*

Arrange the buckling fillets on a serving dish, on a bed of overlapping cucumber slices. Garnish with wedges of lemon.

To make the yoghurt dressing, beat the horseradish sauce into the yoghurt. Stir in the lemon juice and chopped parsley and season with a little salt and black pepper and a pinch of cayenne pepper for piquancy. Serve the sauce separately. Black rye bread is a delicious accompaniment.
*Serves 4*

## Watercress Buns

Choux pastry buns can be filled with a variety of sweet or savoury mixtures. Here, yoghurt cheese and the strong, sharp flavour of watercress combine well. These buns could also be served as a savoury, at the end of a meal, or as a light supper snack.

*65g (2¹/₂ oz) flour*
*¹/₂ teaspoon salt*
*150 ml (¹/₄ pint) water*
*50 g (2 oz) butter*
*2 eggs, beaten*

For filling
*1 bunch watercress, washed and picked over*
*100 g (4 oz) yoghurt cheese (see page 5)*
*1 dessertspoon chopped chives*
*salt*
*freshly-ground black pepper*
*cayenne pepper to garnish*

To make the pastry, sift together the flour and salt. Put the water and butter into a small pan over a low heat until the butter melts. Turn up the heat and bring to the boil. Take the pan off the heat, tip in the sifted flour and beat hard. Gradually add the beaten eggs, a little at a time, and beat well until the mixture is smooth and glossy and leaves the edge of the pan clean.

Using a plain nozzle and a piping bag, pipe 6 rounds of the mixture on to a baking tray. Bake at 220°C(425°F)/Gas 7 for about 20 minutes, until the buns are well risen and golden brown. Transfer the cooked buns to a wire rack and, as soon as they are taken from the oven, split them across one side, to allow the steam to escape.

To make the filling, chop the watercress, reserving a few sprigs to garnish. Put the yoghurt cheese in a bowl and stir in the chopped watercress and chives. Season with salt and pepper.

Pipe the cheese filling into the buns when they are cool. Sprinkle a little cayenne pepper on the top of each one to garnish.
*Makes 6 buns*

## Omelette Ribbons

Sometimes it is more convenient to serve the first course of a meal with the drinks, in which case a selection of 'finger' savouries can be both substantial and interesting. Equally, they can be served at a drinks party – with no meal to follow!

*4 eggs*
*4 tablespoons natural yoghurt*
*salt*
*freshly-ground black pepper*
*1 tablespoon olive oil*
*1 small onion, skinned and chopped*
*1 clove garlic, crushed*
*1 green pepper, trimmed and chopped*
*1 medium-sized potato, cooked, peeled and diced*
*1 thick slice ham, diced*
*4 slices salami, diced*
*4 stuffed green ovlies, sliced*

Lightly beat the eggs and yoghurt together and season well with salt and pepper. Heat the oil in a frying pan and fry the remaining ingredients over a moderate heat for 3–4 minutes. Pour in the egg and yoghurt mixture and tip the pan so that it covers the base. Cook the omelette over moderate-to-high heat for 3 minutes until the underside is lightly browned. Put under a hot grill to cook the top.

Turn the omelette out on to a plate and leave to become cold. Slice it and serve cold, in finger-sized strips, or roll each strip into a pinwheel and secure with a cocktail stick. In this case a cocktail onion rolled into the centre adds interest and 'bite'.
*Makes about 24 slices or wheels*

## Billingsgate Eggs

Hard-boiled eggs piped with seafood filling can be served, as Omelette Ribbons, as an appetiser or on a bed of salad as a complete course. Instead of smoked salmon, you can use canned salmon, tuna fish, crab or anchovies.

*8 eggs, hard boiled and shelled*
*100 g (4 oz) smoked salmon pieces, chopped*
*1/2 teaspoon lemon juice*
*1/4 teaspoon paprika pepper*
*120 ml (4 fl oz) natural yoghurt*
*8 stuffed green olives, halved*

Cut the eggs in half lengthwise and remove the yolks. Put the yolks in a blender with the chopped salmon, lemon juice, paprika and yoghurt and blend for a few seconds. Taste the mixture for seasoning and add more if required.

Fit a star nozzle on to a piping bag and pipe the mixture into the egg-white shells. Garnish each one with half an olive.
*Makes 16 half-eggs*


## Cheese Triangles

More pre-dinner finger-food, an adaption of the Greek *tiropitta*, cheese pies.

*215-g (7 1/2-oz) packet frozen pastry, thawed*
*2 eggs, beaten*
*225 g (8 oz) yoghurt cheese (see page 5)*
*1 dessertspoon fresh chopped parsley*
*salt*
*freshly-ground black pepper*

On a lightly-floured board, roll the pastry out to a rectangle about 38 by 23 cm (15 by 9 ins) and cut into 15 7.5-cm (3-in) squares. Brush along two edges of each square with beaten egg. In a small bowl, beat most of the remaining egg (reserving some to glaze) into the yoghurt cheese. Stir in the parsley and season with salt and pepper.

Divide the mixture between the 15 squares, fold the pastry over to form triangles and pinch the edges to seal. Prick the tops with a fork and brush them with egg. Put the triangles on a wetted baking sheet and bake at 220°C(425°F)/Gas 7 for 10–12 minutes. Serve warm – they reheat very well.
*Makes 15 triangles*


## Cheese Walnuts

Nut-sized balls of chilled cheese can be served on cocktail sticks, kebab style, alternated with whole mushrooms marinated in vinaigrette dressing, baby tomatoes and cubes of celery.

79

*225 g (8 oz) yoghurt cheese (see page 5)*
*1 tablespoon natural yoghurt*
*25 g (1 oz) stuffed green olives, chopped*
*1 teaspoon fresh chopped marjoram* or *parsley*
*salt*
*freshly-ground black pepper*
*50 g (2 oz) walnuts, chopped*

Beat together the yoghurt cheese and the yoghurt and stir in the olives and herbs. Season well with salt and pepper and form into small balls, slightly smaller than a walnut. Roll the balls in the chopped nuts and chill them in the refrigerator. Serve on cocktail sticks.
*Makes about 30*

## Green Avocado Dip

If you keep the prepared dip in a container closely wrapped with clingy film wrap, the dip *will* be green, and stay that way. Serve it with crisp, colourful crudités, matchstick-thin sticks of carrot, celery, green pepper and cucumber, or tiny florets of cauliflower.

*2 avocado pears*
*2 tablespoons white wine vinegar*
*225 g (8 oz) yoghurt cheese (see page 5)*
*1 teaspoon salt*
*1/4 teaspoon cayenne pepper*
*dash of red pepper sauce*
*1 tablespoon onion, finely grated*
*1/2 green pepper, trimmed and finely chopped*

Halve the avocado pears, remove the stones and scoop the flesh from the shells. Put the flesh in a bowl and mash it, then stir in the remaining ingredients. Mix well and cover the container immediately with closely-fitting film wrap. Then the dip can be stored overnight in the refrigerator.
*Makes about 425–450 g (15–16 oz)*

# CHAPTER SIX

# The Centre of Attention

Yoghurt is a traditional and natural ingredient in fish, meat and vegetable dishes originating in Oriental and Middle-Eastern countries. Many of these dishes have become national favourites with us, too.

Cool, bland yoghurt is invaluable for stirring into aromatically spiced sauces, and is the ingredient that blends all the others together. It is a Godsend, too, should a sauce ever turn out to be over-spiced. If the measure of chilli powder proves to be too generous and fiery, a few spoons of yoghurt will do wonders to restore the balance. Yoghurt salad is served as a side dish with many spiced dishes, not so much to cool the palate – though it does – as to provide that contrast that is so important in menu planning.

From the spiced dishes of the Indian Continent to Greece and the Balkans, yoghurt plays its part. In Greece, many meat, vegetable and pasta dishes are topped with a creamy egg, yoghurt and cheese sauce, and in Turkey meat balls – surely more delicious there than anywhere in the world – are presented in a dish of milky-white yoghurt.

The recipes in this chapter, drawn from a wide range of varying cultures, surely prove that yoghurt can be the centre of attention the world over.

## Lima Bean Cake
The beans give a little 'bite' to the smoothness of the courgettes and the creamy yoghurt sauce in this lunch or supper dish.

*225 g (8 oz) dried lima beans, soaked overnight (or use dried white haricot beans)*
*50 g (2 oz) butter*
*1 medium-sized onion, skinned and finely chopped*
*1 clove garlic, peeled and crushed*
*2 tablespoons fresh chopped parsley*
*1/2 teaspoon dried basil*
*2 large tomatoes, skinned and sliced*
*450 g (1 lb) courgettes, washed and sliced*
*salt*
*freshly-ground black pepper*

For sauce
*300 ml (10 fl oz) natural yoghurt*
*2 eggs*
*50 g (2 oz) cheese, grated*

For topping
*50 g (2 oz) dry white breadcrumbs*
*25 g (1 oz) butter, melted*

Cook the soaked lima beans in simmering, unsalted water until tender, about 1 hour. Drain and reserve the liquor. Melt the butter in a large pan, add the onion and garlic and sauté until soft but not turning brown. Add the herbs, stir well, then add the drained cooked beans and 250 ml (1/2 pint) of the reserved liquor. Cover and simmer for about 15 minutes.

Grease a large casserole and arrange alternate layers of the bean mixture with the tomatoes and courgettes, seasoning well between each layer (remember that the beans have been cooked without salt). Cover the casserole closely with a piece of foil, then with the lid, and bake at 150°C(300°F)/Gas 2 for about 1¼ hours.

To make the sauce, beat together the yoghurt and eggs, season well and stir in the cheese. Stir the breadcrumbs into the melted butter. Remove the foil from the casserole, pour on the sauce and top with crumbs. Increase the heat to 190°C(375°F)/Gas 5 and continue to cook the uncovered casserole for a further 25–30 minutes, until the sauce is set and the top crisp and brown.
*Serves 4*

## Lentil Cake
This lentil and vegetable loaf, cut into hearty slices, can be served hot or cold and could well become a family favourite for the vegetarian days when meat just isn't on the menu.

*225 g (8 oz) orange lentils, soaked for at least 1½ hours*
*500 ml (1 pint) water*
*50 g (2 oz) butter*
*1 large onion, skinned and grated*

82

*1 large clove garlic, peeled and crushed*
*2 large tomatoes, skinned and chopped (discard the seeds)*
*1 dessert apple, peeled, cored and grated*
*1 stalk celery, washed and finely chopped*
*50 g (2 oz) wholemeal breadcrumbs*
*75 g (3 oz) shelled walnuts, roughly chopped*
*100 g (4 oz) yoghurt cheese*
*1 tablespoon fresh chopped parsley*
*pinch nutmeg*
*pinch mace*
*salt*
*freshly-ground black pepper*
*2 eggs, well beaten*

Put the soaked lentils in a pan with the water, bring slowly to the boil and simmer for 1 hour. Grease a 450-g (1-lb) loaf tin.

Melt the butter in a pan, add the onion and garlic and sauté over a low heat until transparent. Tip into a bowl, add the cooked lentils – strain them if necessary – and the remaining ingredients except the eggs. Beat well with a wooden spoon. Add the eggs, beat again and knead with the backs of your hands until the mixture is smooth. Pack tightly into the greased loaf tin and stand in a roasting pan containing about 5 cm (2 in) water. Bake in the centre of the oven at 180°C(350°F)/Gas 4 for 45–50 minutes until the top is crunchy and golden brown.

You can serve the loaf hot with colourful vegetables, or cold with salad.
*Serves 4–6*

## Pastitsion
Partly Italian and partly Greek, this pasta dish is served like gingerbread, cut in squares. If there is any left over, it is good cold.

*4 tablespoons olive oil*
*1 medium-sized onion, skinned and chopped*
*1 large clove garlic, peeled and crushed*
*550 g (1¼ lb) minced beef*
*1 396-g (14-oz) can tomatoes*
*1 small wineglass dry white wine*
*2 tablespoons fresh chopped parsley*
*salt*
*freshly-ground black pepper*
*225 g (8 oz) short-cut macaroni*
*40 g (1½ oz) butter*
*2 eggs, beaten*
*3 tablespoons Parmesan cheese, grated*

For sauce
*300 ml (10 fl oz) natural yoghurt*
*2 eggs*
*pinch nutmeg*

Heat the oil in a pan and fry the onion and garlic over a medium heat for 4–5 minutes. Add the minced beef and cook, stirring occasionally, until the meat is light brown. Tip in the can of tomatoes, add the wine and parsley and season well with salt and pepper. Stir over a fairly high heat to reduce the liquid – the mixture should be the consistency of a fairly thick pâté.

Cook the macaroni in plenty of boiling, salted water until it is tender. Drain it and turn in a bowl with the butter. Stir in the beaten eggs.

To make the sauce, beat together the yoghurt and eggs and season well with salt, pepper and nutmeg.

Well grease a gingerbread tin measuring about 25 x 18 x 5 cm (10 x 7 x 2 in). Spread half the pasta over the base of the pan, sprinkle with 1 tablespoon Parmesan cheese and cover with half the meat mixture. Repeat these layers, then pour on the yoghurt sauce and spread it evenly with a knife. Sprinkle on the remaining 1 tablespoon cheese. Bake at 190°C(375°F)/Gas 5 for 20–25 minutes, until the top is golden brown.
*Serves 4–6*


**Aubergine Pasta Pie**
If it weren't for the inclusion of the macaroni, this dish would be a type of moussaka. It has the same delicious 'brown' flavour of aubergine, and a creamy yoghurt topping.

*1 medium-sized aubergine*
*3 tablespoons olive oil*
*1 large onion, skinned and sliced*
*450 g (1 lb) minced beef*
*1 large clove garlic, peeled and crushed*
*salt*
*freshly-ground black pepper*
*1 tablespoon tomato purée*
*1 396-g (14-oz) can tomatoes*
*1 teaspoon dried oregano or basil*
*175 g (6 oz) short-cut macaroni*
*300 ml (10 fl oz) natural yoghurt*
*2 eggs, beaten*
*75 g (3 oz) cheese, grated*

Slice the aubergine diagonally, sprinkle with salt and leave for 30 minutes in a colander to drain. This removes the bitterness from the vegetable. Rinse under the tap and pat dry with kitchen paper. Heat the oil in a heavy pan, fry the aubergine slices until light brown on both sides, remove with a draining spoon and keep warm. Add a little more oil if necessary and fry the onion over a medium heat for 2–3 minutes, then add the minced beef and fry, stirring occasionally, until brown. Add the crushed garlic, seasoning, tomato purée, canned tomatoes and herb and simmer for about 20 minutes. Turn the meat mixture into a 1.5-litre (3-pint) ovenproof dish and arrange the aubergine slices on top.

Cook the macaroni in plenty of boiling, salted water until tender. Drain well.

In a large bowl, combine the yoghurt with the beaten eggs, two-thirds of the grated cheese and the cooked macaroni. Season well and spread over the aubergines. Sprinkle with the remainder of the cheese and bake at 190°C(375°F)/Gas 5 for 25–30 minutes until the top is golden brown.
*Serves 4*


## Vermicelli Flan
The 'pastry' case is vermicelli pressed and baked in a flan ring, and the yoghurt filling has the creamy consistency of a savoury quiche. The contrast of textures makes the flan look good and taste delicious.

*225 g (8 oz) vermicelli*
*25 g (1 oz) butter*
*1 tablespoon olive oil*
*2 medium-sized onions, skinned and chopped*
*175 g (6 oz) bacon rashers, without rind, finely chopped*
*50 g (2 oz) cheese, grated*
*2 eggs*
*150 ml (5 fl oz) natural yoghurt*
*salt*
*freshly-ground black pepper*
*1 teaspoon dried basil or oregano*
*3 large tomatoes, thinly sliced*
*melted butter to glaze*

Cook the vermicelli in plenty of boiling, salted water until it is just tender. Drain and, while it is still warm, toss with the butter until well coated. Press the mixture into a 20-cm (8-in) flan ring on a baking sheet.

Heat the oil in a frying pan and fry the onion and bacon for 3–4 minutes over a medium heat. Spread the grated cheese over the pasta case and sprinkle on the onion and bacon mixture. Beat the eggs and yoghurt together and season with salt, pepper and dried herb. Pour the mixture into the flan case and arrange the tomatoes in overlapping rings around the outside of the flan, to cover the pasta. Grind some black pepper over the tomatoes, sprinkle with a little extra dried herb, and brush with melted butter. Bake at 180°C(350°F)/Gas 4 for 40–45

minutes until the filling is set. Slide the flan on to a serving plate and remove the flan ring. Serve hot with a green salad.
*Serves 4*

## Pasta with Veal Sauce
The sauce is well flavoured with vegetables and herbs, and the topping smooth and cheesy.

*2 tablespoons vegetable oil*
*1 large onion, skinned and sliced*
*1 large carrot, peeled or scraped and sliced*
*2 stalks celery, washed and chopped*
*1 green pepper, trimmed and sliced*
*1 clove garlic, peeled and crushed*
*450 g (1 lb) minced veal*
*1 tablespoon tomato purée*
*1 396-g (14-oz) can tomatoes*
*1 teaspoon dried oregano or basil*
*salt*
*freshly-ground black pepper*
*175 g (6 oz) short-cut pasta, such as macaroni*
*300 ml (10 fl oz) natural yoghurt*
*2 eggs*
*75 g (3 oz) cheese, grated*

Heat the oil in a pan, add the onion, carrot, celery, green pepper and garlic and fry over a moderate heat for 3–4 minutes, until the onion becomes transparent. Add the meat and fry, stirring, until it lightly browns. Add the tomato purée, canned tomatoes and dried herb, and season well with salt and pepper. Stir, cover the pan and simmer for 20 minutes.

Cook the pasta in plenty of boiling, salted water, according to the instructions on the packet, until it is just tender. Drain the pasta well. Beat together the yoghurt and eggs and stir into the pasta. Add two-thirds of the cheese and season lightly with salt and pepper.

Pour the meat mixture into an ovenproof dish, cover with the yoghurt sauce and sprinkle with the remaining cheese. Bake at 190°C(375°F)/Gas 5 for 25–30 minutes, until the sauce is brown and bubbling.
*Serves 4*

## Spiced Pasta Chicken
Cooked chicken presented in a tangy sauce on a bed of pasta.

*75 g (3 oz) butter*
*1 large onion, skinned and chopped*

*1 teaspoon ground turmeric*
*1 teaspoon garam masala*
*¹/₄ teaspoon ground cloves*
*¹/₄ teaspoon ground cumin seed*
*¹/₄ teaspoon freshly-ground black pepper*
*¹/₈ teaspoon chilli powder*
*¹/₈ teaspoon ground ginger*
*40 g (1¹/₂ oz) flour*
*600 ml (1 pint) whey (see page 5) or chicken stock*
*2 tablespoons mango chutney, chopped*
*450 g (1 lb) chicken, cooked and diced*
*25 g (1 oz) sultanas*
*225 g (8 oz) short-cut pasta (spirals or shells)*
*150 ml (5 fl oz) natural yoghurt*

Melt two-thirds of the butter in a frying pan, add the onion and fry for 3–4 minutes over a moderate heat, stirring occasionally. Add all the spices and the flour and stir for 1 minute. Gradually pour on the stock, stirring, add the mango chutney and bring the sauce to the boil. Cover and simmer for 15 minutes. Add the chicken and sultanas to the sauce, stir well and simmer for a further 5 minutes.

Meanwhile cook the pasta in plenty of boiling, salted water according to the directions on the packet. When it is just tender, drain it and toss it with the remaining butter. Turn the pasta into a heated serving dish. Stir the yoghurt into the chicken mixture and spoon it over the pasta.
*Serves 4*


## Chicken Ginger
A spiced sauce to make chicken joints rather special.

*25 g (1 oz) butter*
*1 tablespoon oil*
*4 chicken joints, skinned*
*salt*
*freshly-ground black pepper*
*¹/₂ teaspoon ground ginger*
*1 medium-sized onion, skinned and chopped*
*2 stalks celery, washed and chopped*
*1 red pepper, trimmed and chopped*
*1 green pepper, trimmed and chopped*
*300 ml (¹/₂ pint) chicken stock or water and stock cube*
*50 g (2 oz) stem ginger, chopped*
*50 g (2 oz) button mushrooms, wiped and trimmed*

2 tablespoons cornflour
4 tablespoons water
450 ml (15 fl oz) natural yoghurt
1 tablespoon fresh chopped parsley to garnish

Melt the butter and oil in a large pan. Season the chicken joints with salt, pepper and ground ginger and fry them for 5–6 minutes on each side until they are golden brown. Remove the chicken joints and keep them hot. Add the onion, celery, red and green pepper to the fat in the pan and fry, stirring occasionally, for 3 minutes. Gradually pour in the stock, and stir until it boils. Add the chopped ginger and the mushrooms and return the chicken to the pan. Cover the pan and simmer for 1 hour, until the chicken is cooked. Remove the chicken and keep hot.

Put the cornflour in a small bowl, pour on the water and stir to make a smooth paste. Pour over a little of the chicken stock from the pan, then pour the paste into the pan to thicken the sauce. Bring to the boil, stirring, and boil for 1 minute. Stir in most of the yoghurt and heat without boiling.

Put the chicken joints on a heated dish, pour over the sauce and top with the reserved yoghurt. Sprinkle with the parsley.
*Serves 4*


## Balkan Chicken

By the time the chicken and shallots have taken up the flavour of the wine, and the yoghurt mellows the sauce, you have a dish fit for any occasion.

2 small chickens (poussins)
juice of 1/2 lemon
50 g (2 oz) butter
6 shallots, skinned and left whole
125 ml (scant 1/4 pint) dry white wine or dry sherry
salt
freshly-ground black pepper

For sauce
125 ml (1/4 pint) dry white wine or dry sherry
6 shallots, skinned
25 g (1 oz) butter
25 g (1 oz) flour
150 ml (5 fl oz) natural yoghurt
1 tablespoon fresh chopped parsley to garnish

Wipe the birds thoroughly with a clean, damp cloth and rub them all over with lemon juice. Melt the butter in a flameproof casserole and brown the birds on all sides. Add the shallots and wine, season well with salt and pepper, cover and cook at 180°C(350°F)/Gas 4 for 30–40 minutes, until the birds are tender. Pour off the stock and reserve it, and keep the birds hot.

To make the sauce, pour the wine into a small saucepan and add the shallots. Reduce the wine volume by half over a fairly high heat, and set aside. Melt the butter in a small pan, stir in the flour and cook over a medium heat, stirring, for 1 minute. Gradually stir in the stock in which the chicken has been cooked and the reduced wine, including all the shallots. Bring to the boil and simmer, stirring, for 2 minutes. Add the yoghurt and reheat gently; do not allow to boil.

Split the poussins in half and arrange in a casserole. Pour the sauce over them and sprinkle with the chopped parsley to garnish. Serve with buttered noodles.
*Serves 4*

## Tarragon Chicken

Only half an hour after coming in, you can have this dish on the table, golden chicken in a sauce fragrant with wine and herbs. If you do not have fresh tarragon, substitute fresh marjoram, thyme or even mint, combined with the parsley. Dried herbs are not really suitable.

*4 wing joints of chicken*
*juice of ¹/₂ lemon*
*25 g (1 oz) butter*
*70 ml (¹/₈ pint) dry white wine or dry cider*
*210 ml (³/₈ pint) chicken stock*
*1 tablespoon fresh chopped parsley*
*1 tablespoon fresh chopped tarragon or other herb (see note above)*
*1 large clove garlic, peeled and crushed*
*salt*
*freshly-ground black pepper*
*150 ml (5 fl oz) natural yoghurt*

For topping
*50 g (2 oz) butter*
*75 g (3 oz) fresh white breadcrumbs*

Cut the small wing-bone joint from the chicken pieces and discard. Rub the lemon juice into the meat. Heat the butter in a frying pan and fry the chicken joints for a few minutes on each side until light brown. Pour in the wine or cider and stock and bring to the boil. Add the herbs and garlic and season well with salt and pepper. Simmer for 20 minutes, remove from the heat and then stir in the yoghurt. Reheat the sauce, without boiling. Transfer the chicken pieces to a heated serving dish and pour the sauce over them. Sprinkle with the buttered crumbs and serve with green noodles.

To prepare the buttered crumbs, heat the butter in a small pan, stir in the breadcrumbs and fry until golden brown and dry.
*Serves 4*

## Chicken Turmeric

A golden, lightly spiced sauce to dress up everyday chicken joints.

*3 tablespoons vegetable oil*
*1 green pepper, trimmed and sliced*
*1 large onion, skinned and chopped*
*1 clove garlic, peeled and crushed*
*1 teaspoon ground turmeric*
*¼ teaspoon ground ginger*
*¼ teaspoon ground cardamom seeds*
*4 chicken joints, skinned*
*1 tablespoon clear honey*
*2 tablespoons whey (see page 5) or water, warm*
*¼ teaspoon salt*
*¼ teaspoon freshly-ground black pepper*
*150 ml (5 fl oz) natural yoghurt*

Heat the oil in a pan and add the chopped pepper, onion and garlic. Stir in the turmeric, ginger and cardamom, mix well and fry over a low heat for 2–3 minutes. Add the chicken joints and fry for 3–4 minutes on each side, so that they brown slightly. Stir the honey into the warm liquid and add to the pan with the salt and pepper. Cover the pan and cook over a low heat for 30 minutes, turning the chicken joints once during this time. Stir in the yoghurt and heat gently.

Serve with plain boiled rice.

*Serves 4*

## Chicken Cutlets with Mushroom Sauce

These cutlets, formed from a sauce made of minced meat and double cream, are tricky – and sticky – to handle. The secret is to toss them quickly from one hand to the other. It helps to hold your hands under cold running water first.

*675 g (1½ lb) cooked chicken, finely minced 2 or 3 times*
*salt*
*freshly-ground black pepper*
*180 ml (6 fl oz) double cream, chilled*
*flour to dust*
*40 g (1½ oz) butter*
*225 g (8 oz) button mushrooms, wiped and thinly sliced*
*1 tablespoon flour*
*150 ml (¼ pint) dry white wine*
*300 ml (10 fl oz) natural yoghurt*
*1 teaspoon dill seed*

Put the minced chicken in a bowl and pound it smooth with a pestle or the back of a tablespoon. Season it well with salt and pepper and beat in the double cream.

Continue beating until a smooth paste is formed. Dust your hands with flour and shape the mixture into eight small rounds.

Melt two-thirds of the butter in a pan and carefully lower in the cutlets, using a fish slice. Fry them over medium heat for 3–4 minutes on each side, until they begin to 'sweat'. Remove the cutlets from the pan and arrange them on a serving dish.

Add the remaining butter to the pan and fry the mushrooms for about 2 minutes, until they are just beginning to soften. Sprinkle on 1 level tablespoon flour and cook, stirring, for 1 minute. Gradually pour on first the wine and then the yoghurt and cook, stirring, until the sauce thickens. Season well and pour over the cutlets. Serve at once, with boiled rice.
*Serves 4–6*

## Chicken and Corn Fritters
Here the traditional flavour combination of chicken, corn and banana is presented in a new way.

*25 g (1 oz) butter*
*1 medium-sized onion, skinned and chopped*
*25 g (1 oz) flour*
*300 ml (½ pint) milk*
*225 g (8 oz) chicken, cooked and diced*
*1 200-g (7-oz) can sweetcorn, drained*
*½ teaspoon mustard powder*
*1 tablespoon fresh chopped parsley*
*½ teaspoon salt*
*freshly-ground black pepper*

For batter
*175 g (6 oz) flour*
*¼ teaspoon salt*
*150 ml (¼ pint) light ale*
*4 tablespoons water*
*oil for frying*

For sauce
*300 ml (10 fl oz) natural yoghurt, chilled*
*2 bananas*
*pinch cayenne pepper*
*salt*

To make the fritters, melt the butter in a pan and fry the chopped onion for 3–4 minutes over moderate heat, until it is softened. Sprinkle on the flour and cook, stirring, for 1 minute. Remove the pan from the heat, gradually pour on the milk, still stirring, then cook over a low heat until the sauce thickens. Allow the sauce to cool, then stir in the chicken, sweetcorn, mustard powder, parsley and seasoning. Beat the mixture well. Dust your hands with flour and shape the mixture into eight oblongs or rounds.

To make the batter, mix the flour and salt together in a bowl and gradually pour on half the beer. Beat well, then beat in the remaining beer and the water.

Heat enough oil in a pan for shallow frying. Dip the fritters into the batter, allowing any excess batter to drain from them, then fry for 4–5 minutes on each side, until the fritters are golden brown. Arrange them on a heated serving dish.

To make the sauce, put the yoghurt, bananas and seasoning in a blender and blend until smooth, or mash the bananas in a bowl and beat the yoghurt and seasoning. Serve the sauce separately. A crisp salad such as chicory and watercress goes well with this dish.
*Serves 4*


## Lamb with Lemon Sauce

The traditional stand-by of Greek cooking, egg and lemon sauce enriches the wine and herb stock in which the meat is cooked. And, bending tradition a little, yoghurt makes a bland and perfect topping.

*4 tablespoons oil*
*900 g (2 lb) lean lamb, trimmed and cut into 2.5-cm (1-in) cubes*
*1 small onion, skinned and chopped*
*1 clove garlic, peeled and crushed*
*1 tablespoon flour*
*2 large tomatoes, skinned and chopped*
*150 ml (¼ pint) dry white wine*
*450 ml (¾ pint) chicken stock, hot*
*salt*
*freshly-ground black pepper*
*1 bayleaf*
*1 teaspoon dried basil or oregano*
*150 ml (5 fl oz) natural yoghurt to serve*

For egg and lemon sauce
*2 egg yolks*
*juice of 1 lemon*
*1 tablespoon fresh chopped parsley to garnish*

Heat the oil in a flameproof casserole and brown the meat a few cubes at a time. Remove the meat with a draining spoon, set aside to keep warm, and fry the onion and garlic in the oil for 4–5 minutes over a medium heat. Sprinkle on the flour and stir in the chopped tomatoes. Pour in the white wine and hot chicken stock, season well with salt and pepper and add the bayleaf and herb. Bring to the

92

boil, stirring, return the meat to the casserole and cover. Cook at 180°C(350°F)/Gas 4, for 1–1¼ hours.

Using a draining spoon, transfer the meat to a serving dish. Strain the stock into a small pan. Beat together the egg yolks and strained lemon juice and stir in 4 tablespoons of the stock. Whisk the egg mixture into the strained stock in the pan and re-heat without boiling. Pour the sauce over the meat, spoon the yoghurt on top and garnish with the chopped parsley. Serve with boiled new potatoes.
*Serves 4*

## Lamb with Green Pickles
The sweetness of the meat takes well to a sauce sharpened with green pickles.

*25 g (1 oz) butter*
*1 tablespoon vegetable oil*
*1 large onion, skinned and chopped*
*675 g (1½ lb) lean lamb, cut into 2.5-cm (1-in) cubes*
*25 g (1 oz) flour*
*300 ml (½ pint) whey (see page 5) or chicken stock*
*salt*
*freshly-ground black pepper*
*1 green pepper, trimmed and chopped*
*1 tablespoon capers, rinsed in cold water*
*2 small gherkins, rinsed and sliced*
*1 pickled dill cucumber, rinsed and sliced*
*grated zest of 1 lemon*
*1 tablespoon fresh chopped parsley*
*300 ml (10 fl oz) natural yoghurt*

Melt the butter and oil in a large pan and fry the onion over a moderate heat for 4–5 minutes until it becomes transparent but not brown. Add the cubes of lamb and fry for a further 3 minutes, stirring to make sure the meat is sealed on all sides. Add the flour and cook, stirring, for 1 minute, then gradually pour on the liquid. Bring to the boil, stirring, season well and add the green pepper, capers, pickles, lemon zest and chopped parsley. Cover the pan and simmer for 1–1¼ hours, until the meat is tender. Stir in the yoghurt and heat gently without boiling. Taste for seasoning and, if you like, add a pinch of sugar. Serve with boiled potatoes.
*Serves 4*

## Lamb Chops with Ham Sauce
With a large parcel of lamb chops in the freezer, I am constantly searching for new ideas. This combination of lamb, yoghurt and ham is interesting and uncomplicated.

*4 lamb chump chops, trimmed of excess fat*
*salt*
*freshly-ground black pepper*
*50 g (2 oz) butter*
*1 medium-sized onion, skinned and chopped*
*1 clove garlic, peeled and crushed*
*15 g (¹/₂ oz) flour*
*300 ml (10 fl oz) natural yoghurt*
*100 g (4 oz) ham, trimmed of fat and diced*

Season the chops with salt and pepper. Melt half the butter in a frying pan and fry the chops over a moderate heat for 4–5 minutes on each side, until they are brown. Transfer the chops to an ovenproof casserole and keep them warm.

Add the remainder of the butter to the pan and fry the onion and garlic over medium heat for 3–4 minutes. Stir in the flour, mix thoroughly, remove the pan from the heat, then gradually stir in the yoghurt. Slowly bring the sauce to simmering point over a low heat, then season with salt and pepper and purée in a blender. Without a blender, press the sauce through a sieve; this way you will retain less of the onion flavour. Add the ham to the sauce and spread it over the chops. Cook at 180°C(350°F)/Gas 4 for 20 minutes. Serve with a green vegetable such as French beans or whole courgettes.
*Serves 4*

### Pink Lamb Casserole
Lightly spiced with paprika pepper, the lamb is served in a tomato and yoghurt sauce.

*1.25 kg (2¹/₂ lb) lean lamb, cubed*
*¹/₂ teaspoon salt*
*¹/₄ teaspoon freshly-ground black pepper*
*1 dessertspoon paprika pepper*
*40 g (1¹/₂ oz) butter*
*1 large onion, skinned and sliced*
*1 red pepper, trimmed and thinly sliced*
*1 396-g (14-oz) can tomatoes, chopped*
*1 tablespoon tomato purée*
*1 bayleaf*
*75 ml (2¹/₂ fl oz) natural yoghurt*
*1 tablespoon fresh chopped dill leaves* or *parsley to garnish*

Put the cubed lamb into a greaseproof or polythene bag with salt, black pepper and paprika pepper and shake to coat the meat.

Melt the butter in a pan, add the meat and fry over a moderate heat, stirring from time to time, to brown on all sides. Transfer the meat to an ovenproof casserole and keep it warm.

Add the onion and red pepper to the fat in the pan and fry for 4–5 minutes, stirring at least once. Add the chopped tomatoes with the liquid from the can and the tomato purée and stir over the heat to blend well. Pour the tomato mixture over the meat, add the bayleaf and stir so that the meat will not stick. Cover the casserole and cook at 150°C(300°)/Gas 2 for 2–2½ hours until the meat is tender. Remove the bayleaf. Stir in the yoghurt and return to the oven for a few minutes to heat.

Serve sprinkled with fresh herbs.

*Serves 4–6*


## Spiced Leg of Lamb

The tenderest way to cook lamb – it is first marinated in yoghurt dressing, then spread with a spicy yoghurt paste.

*1.75-kg (4-lb) leg of lamb, boned and tied*
*3 cloves garlic, peeled and sliced*
*juice of 2 lemons*
*600 ml (20 fl oz) natural yoghurt*
*1 teaspoon fresh chopped basil* or *marjoram*
*1 teaspoon ground cumin seed*
*1 teaspoon ground coriander*
*½ teaspoon ground turmeric*
*pinch grated nutmeg*
*¼ teaspoon salt*
*¼ teaspoon freshly-ground black pepper*
*5 tablespoons oil for cooking*

Make slits in the lamb with a sharp-pointed knife and insert the strips of garlic. Put the lamb in a large bowl or plastic container. Mix together the lemon juice and yoghurt, pour over the lamb and turn the meat in the marinade. Cover the container and leave in the refrigerator or a cold place, turning the meat occasionally, for 24 hours.

To make the paste, mix together the fresh herb, the spices, salt and pepper. Measure 150 ml (5 fl oz) of the yoghurt marinade (reserve the rest for another dish) and blend it thoroughly into the spice mixture.

Pour the oil in a roasting pan. Wipe the meat dry with kitchen paper and cover it all over with the yoghurt paste. Put the meat in the pan, baste it with the oil and cook at 180°C(350°F)/Gas 4 for 2 hours, until the meat is cooked. Baste the meat from time to time, during cooking, and turn it at least once so that it is evenly crisp.

Serve the meat with plain boiled rice or a pilaf and Mint and Garlic sauce (see next recipe).

*Serves 6–8*

## Mint and Garlic Sauce

*300 ml (10 fl oz) natural yoghurt*
*¹/₂ teaspoon salt*
*2–3 cloves garlic, peeled and crushed*
*1 tablespoon fresh, finely-chopped mint*

Put a little yoghurt in a bowl, add the salt and crushed garlic and pound to a smooth paste. Gradually stir in the rest of the yoghurt, then the mint, and beat until the sauce is smooth. Store in a covered container in the refrigerator or a cold place. The flavour improves with keeping, so if possible the sauce should be made the day before it is needed.
*Makes 300 ml (10 fl oz) sauce*


## Tikka Kebabs

As the meat needs to be prepared a day in advance and left to infuse in the spicy marinade, this is a good dish to plan for a busy day. The last-minute assembly and cooking time is minimal.

*450 g (1 lb) lean lamb, cut into 2.5-cm (1-in) cubes*
*oil for brushing*
*175 g (6 oz) button mushrooms, wiped and trimmed*
*12 small onions, skinned and blanched in boiling, salted water for 5 minutes*
*1 green pepper, trimmed and cut into 2.5-cm (1-in) squares*
*8 small tomatoes*
*4 bayleaves*
*2 lemons, quartered*

For marinade
*300 ml (10 fl oz) natural yoghurt*
*1 teaspoon garam masala*
*1 teaspoon ground coriander*
*¹/₂ teaspoon ground turmeric*
*¹/₂ teaspoon ground cumin seed*
*¹/₂ teaspoon salt*
*¹/₄ teaspoon freshly-grated nutmeg*
*¹/₄ teaspoon chilli powder*
*grated zest and juice of 1 lemon*

Put the ingredients for the marinade into a shallow dish, stir well and add the lamb cubes. Mix well, cover and leave in a cool place overnight, or for about 12 hours, stirring occasionally if it is convenient.

Remove the lamb, using a draining spoon, and reserve the marinade. Brush 4 kebab skewers with oil and thread them with pieces of lamb, whole mushrooms, onions, green pepper slices, tomatoes and bayleaves. Arrange the meat and vegetables so that you achieve a good balance of colour and texture.

Line a grill pan with foil, turn the grill heat to high and arrange the skewers on the pan. Turn the heat down to moderate and grill the skewers for about 20 minutes, turning them once, until the meat is cooked and tender.

Heat the yoghurt marinade in a small pan without boiling and serve separately, as a sauce.

Serve the skewers on a bed of plain, boiled rice, garnished with the lemon wedges.
*Serves 4*

## Pork Paprika
Paprika pepper and yoghurt are natural partners, blending into a mild, rosy sauce – especially good, here, with pork chops.

> *1 tablespoon vegetable oil*
> *4 pork chops, trimmed of fat and bone*
> *salt*
> *freshly-ground pepper*
> *1 medium-sized onion, skinned and sliced*
> *1 large red pepper, trimmed and chopped or 1 canned pimento, drained and chopped*
> *1 tablespoon paprika pepper*
> *1 65-g (2¹/₂-oz) can tomato purée*
> *150 ml (¹/₄ pint) whey (see page 5) or chicken stock, hot*
> *100 g (4 oz) button mushrooms, wiped, trimmed and sliced*
> *300 ml (10 fl oz) natural yoghurt*

Heat the oil in a pan. Season the pork chops with salt and pepper and fry them for 4–5 minutes on each side over a medium-to-high heat to seal. Remove the chops from the pan and keep them hot. Add the onion and red pepper to the oil in the pan and fry gently for 3–4 minutes, then sprinkle on the paprika pepper and stir well. Stir the tomato purée into the hot whey or stock and gradually pour it into the pan, stirring until the sauce boils. Return the pork chops to the pan, cover and simmer for 1 hour, until the meat is cooked. Add the sliced mushrooms and cook for a further 5 minutes, then stir in half the yoghurt. Heat gently, without boiling; pour over the remainder of the yoghurt to garnish.
*Serves 4*

## January Pork
A hint of cider and sherry add interest to this dish in which cabbage and pork are cooked together.

> *675 g (1¹/₂ lb) cabbage*
> *40 g (1¹/₂ oz) butter*

*1 large onion, skinned and finely chopped*
*1 clove garlic, peeled and crushed*
*1 teaspoon caraway seeds*
*salt*
*freshly-ground black pepper*
*4 pork chops, trimmed of excess fat*
*300 ml (¹/₂ pint) dry cider*
*2 tablespoons dry sherry*
*150 ml (5 fl oz) natural yoghurt*
*50 g (2 oz) cheese, grated*

Wash the cabbage, shred it finely and cook it in boiling, salted water for 5 minutes. Drain it thoroughly and turn it into a large bowl. Melt two-thirds of the butter in a frying pan and fry the onion and garlic over a moderate heat for 4–5 minutes until the onion is transparent. Add the onion mixture to the cabbage and stir in the caraway seeds. Season well. Turn half the cabbage mixture into an ovenproof casserole.

Heat the remaining butter in the frying pan and fry the pork chops over a medium-to-high heat, turning once, until they are brown on both sides. Arrange them over the cabbage layer in the casserole and season them with salt and pepper. Spread the remainder of the cabbage over the chops.

Pour the cider and sherry into the frying pan and reduce the liquid over a moderate heat until there are about 5–6 tablespoons left. Remove the pan from the heat and stir in the yoghurt to blend well. Pour the sauce over the cabbage, cover the casserole and cook at 180°C(350°F)/Gas 4 for 45 minutes. Remove the casserole from the oven, sprinkle the cheese on top and return it to the oven, uncovered, to cook for a further 20-25 minutes, until the chesse is golden brown. Serve with a purée of potatoes.
*Serves 4*


**Yoghurt Steak Tartare**
Try the addition of yoghurt to the dressing of this classic uncooked dish. It blends well with the sharpness of the accompanying flavourings.

*450 g (1 lb) lean rump steak, finely minced 2 or 3 times*
*4 tablespoons natural yoghurt, chilled*
*4 egg yolks*
*1 small onion, skinned and cut into rings*
*freshly-ground black pepper*
*salt*
*100 g (4 oz) capers, drained and chopped*
*4 tablespoons fresh chopped parsley*
*1 can anchovy fillets, drained and finely chopped*

Mince the steak just before serving. If it is prepared well in advance it will lose the freshness of colour essential to this dish. Divide the minced steak between 4 plates. Shape the meat into rounds, then, with the back of a tablespoon, push a hole in the centre of each round. Pour 1 tablespoon of yoghurt into each well and carefully slide an egg yolk on top of the yoghurt. Garnish each portion with a few onion rings.

Serve the remaining ingredients on separate saucers, or in cocotte dishes. The pepper, salt, capers, parsley and anchovies are all mixed with the steak to the individual taste of each diner.

Do not serve other vegetables or salads with this dish. Thinly sliced bread and butter is all that is needed.
*Serves 4*

## Beef 'Yoganoff'
A yoghurt version of the traditional nineteenth-century Russian dish.

*4 tablespoons vegetable oil*
*2 large onions, skinned and cut into rings*
*450 g (1 lb) mushrooms, wiped and thinly sliced*
*1 kg (2 lb) fillet of beef, trimmed of fat*
*1/2 teaspoon salt*
*freshly-ground black pepper*
*1 teaspoon sugar*
*1 tablespoon made mustard*
*300 ml (10 fl oz) natural yoghurt*

Heat 1 tablespoon of the oil in a heavy-based frying pan and fry the onions and mushrooms in the covered pan for 20 minutes over a low heat. Remove the vegetables with a draining spoon, pour away the liquid and return the onions and mushrooms to the dry pan.

With a very sharp knife, cut the steak into match-stick lengths about 0.5 cm (1/4 in) wide. Heat 1 1/2 tablespoons of the oil in a second heavy pan and fry half the beef for 2 minutes. Stir the meat constantly with a wooden spoon to brown it on all sides. Transfer the cooked meat to the pan with the vegetables, add the remaining oil to the second pan and fry the remainder of the meat. Transfer this to the vegetable pan and, using a wooden spoon, stir in the salt, pepper, sugar and mustard. Gradually stir in the yoghurt and allow the sauce to heat through over a low heat for 2–3 minutes. Taste and adjust the seasoning if necessary.

Serve the beef on a heated dish, surrounded by a ring of plain boiled rice.

Do not be tempted to substitute a cheaper cut of meat for the fillet steak; it does not work!
*Serves 4*

## Mustard Veal

The delicate flavour of this mustard sauce does great things for veal!

*2 tablespoons vegetable oil*
*4 veal chops*
*100 g (4 oz) streaky bacon, de-rinded and chopped*
*2 large onions, skinned and sliced*
*1 tablespoon flour*
*180 ml (just over ¼ pint) chicken stock, hot*
*1 bayleaf*
*salt*
*freshly-ground black pepper*
*150 ml (5 fl oz) natural yoghurt*
*2 tablespoons Meaux mustard*
*a little extra yoghurt to garnish*
*1 tablespoon fresh chopped chives to garnish*

Heat the vegetable oil in a frying pan and brown the chops on both sides over a medium heat. Transfer the chops to an ovenproof casserole. Add the bacon and the onion to the pan and fry over a moderate heat until the bacon fat runs and the onions are transparent. Sprinkle on the flour, stir well and gradually pour on the stock. Stir over the heat until the sauce boils. Add the bayleaf, season with salt and pepper and pour over the chops. Cover the casserole and cook at 180°C(350°F)/Gas 4 for 1 hour, until the chops are cooked. Remove the bayleaf.

Mix together the yoghurt and mustard, stir into the sauce and return to the oven to heat through. Garnish with a spoonful of natural yoghurt and the chopped chives.
*Serves 4*


## Hungarian Goulash

This is basic casserole cookery, a good country dish that is perfect for a winter buffet party.

*25 g (1 oz) white vegetable fat*
*1 large onion, skinned and finely chopped*
*2 cloves garlic, peeled and finely chopped*
*2 tablespoons paprika pepper*
*1 kg (2 lb) stewing steak, trimmed of fat and cut into cubes*
*½ teaspoon caraway seeds*
*750 ml (1¼ pints) brown stock (or use water and stock cube), hot*
*450 g (1 lb) potatoes, peeled and diced*
*450 g (1 lb) tomatoes, skinned and chopped*
*2 green peppers, trimmed and sliced*

*1 tablespoon fresh chopped marjoram*
*salt*
*freshly-ground black pepper*
*150 ml (5 fl oz) natural yoghurt*

Heat the fat in a large saucepan and fry the onion and garlic over a moderate heat for 5–6 minutes, until they are light brown. Stir in the paprika and cook for 1 minute. Add the meat and caraway seeds, stir well, and gradually pour on the stock, stirring. Bring slowly to the boil, cover the pan and simmer for 1 hour. Add the potatoes, tomatoes, peppers and marjoram and season with salt and black pepper. Cover the pan and continue cooking for a further 45 minutes, until the potatoes are cooked. Stir in the yoghurt, and heat gently.

Serve with buttered noodles with a few caraway seeds stirred in.
*Serves 4–6*

## Ragout of Liver
This is a good way to turn a relatively small amount of meat into a substantial winter casserole.

*450 g (1 lb) lambs' liver, very thinly sliced*
*1 large onion, skinned and chopped*
*2 medium-sized carrots, peeled or scraped and diced*
*1 large parsnip, peeled and diced*
*2 small turnips, peeled and diced*
*600 ml (1 pint) brown beef stock (or use yoghurt whey – see page 5 – or water and a*
*    stock cube)*
*100 g (4 oz) belly of pork, roughly chopped*
*1 teaspoon Worcestershire sauce*
*salt*
*freshly-ground black pepper*
*300 ml (10 fl oz) natural yoghurt*
*1 tablespoon fresh chopped parsley*

Blanch the sliced liver in boiling, salted water for 1 minute and drain, discarding the liquid. Put the prepared vegetables into a large flameproof casserole with the stock, pork, Worcestershire sauce and seasoning. Cover, bring to the boil and simmer gently for about 40 minutes until the vegetables are tender. Add the sliced liver and simmer for a further 10–15 minutes, depending on the thickness, until the liver is cooked. Stir in three-quarters of the yoghurt and blend well into the stock. Allow the sauce to heat but not boil.

To serve, spoon the remaining yoghurt over the meat, and sprinkle with chopped parsley. Serve with a green vegetable such as broccoli or brussels sprouts.
*Serves 4*

**Fisherman's Stew**

This dish improves if made a day in advance and left, covered, in the refrigerator while the flavours mellow and blend.

*3 tablespoons olive oil*
*2 large onions, skinned and sliced*
*4 cloves garlic, peeled and chopped*
*2 375-g (14-oz) cans tomatoes*
*1* bouquet garni *of mixed herbs*
*900 ml (1 ½ pints) fish stock, hot (made from fish trimmings, an onion and a bunch of herbs)*
*salt*
*freshly-ground black pepper*
*450 g (1 lb) potatoes, peeled and diced*
*1 kg (2 lb) white fish (cod, haddock, coley) skinned and boned*

For sauce
*150 ml (5 fl oz) natural yoghurt*
*2 cloves garlic, peeled and crushed*
*½ teaspoon salt*

Heat the oil in a flameproof casserole or a pan and fry the onion and garlic over a low heat for 4–5 minutes. Add the tomatoes and *bouquet garni* and cook, stirring occasionally, until the tomatoes are soft. Pour on the hot, strained fish stock, bring to simmering point and simmer for 15 minutes. Season with salt and pepper and add the potatoes. Cover and cook for 20 minutes, then add the fish, broken into large chunks. Simmer for 10 minutes until the fish is just cooked – overcooking will toughen it. Remove the *bouquet garni*.

To make the sauce, put a little of the yoghurt in a bowl, blend in the crushed garlic and the salt to make a paste, then stir in the rest of the yoghurt. Season well with pepper.

Serve the stew piping hot, in deep soup plates, with a spoonful of garlic sauce in the centre of each. Fingers of toast are a good accompaniment.
*Serves 6*


**Prawns in Yoghurt Sauce**

The simplest methods of cooking are often the best. This way of preparing prawns retains almost all the flavour, and the yoghurt sauce merely enhances it.

*1 litre (2 pints) fresh prawns*
*300 ml (10 fl oz) natural yoghurt*
*grated zest and juice of 1 lemon*
*pinch cayenne pepper*

*freshly-ground black pepper*
*1 tablespoon capers, drained and rinsed*
*lemon wedges to serve*

Thoroughly wash the prawns in several bowls of fresh water until all the grit is removed. Drain them and put them in a large pan. Cover the pan and set it over a low heat so that the prawns sweat slowly. Shake the pan to prevent sticking and ensure even cooking. The prawns should be cooked in 10–12 minutes. Remove the pan from the heat, allow the prawns to cool a little, then shell them. Reserve a few unshelled ones to garnish.

Put the yoghurt in a bowl and whip it, then stir in the remaining ingredients. Pour the yoghurt sauce into a serving bowl and stand it in the centre of a large plate. Arrange the shelled prawns around the bowl and garnish with whole prawns and lemon wedges. Serve with a green salad and rye bread for a light supper.
*Serves 4*


## Tomato Soufflé

A soufflé is a wonderful way of serving vegetables, transforming them into a high, light concoction that will certainly be the focal point of a meal. I like to make soufflés with root vegetables such as Jerusalem artichokes or celeriac – 300 ml (½ pint) of vegetable purée to the basic sauce mixture (see below) – and with imported vegetables such as aubergines, to make a little go a long way. I use this soufflé recipe when tomatoes are expensive in the shops or when I'm running out of ideas to utilize a garden glut. Serve the soufflé with a crisp green salad, such as chicory, green pepper and onion, and hot garlic bread.

*75 g (3 oz) butter*
*50 g (2 oz) flour, sifted*
*300 ml (½ pint) milk, warm*
*300 ml (½ pint) strained tomato pulp*
*1 teaspoon tomato purée*
*3 large eggs, separated, and 1 extra egg white*
*120 ml (4 fl oz) natural yoghurt*
*salt*
*freshly-ground black pepper*
*pinch dried basil*
*1 clove garlic, peeled*
*olive oil*

Melt the butter in a heavy pan over a low heat. Stir in the flour and gradually pour in the milk, stirring all the time. Bring the sauce to boiling point, still stirring, and cook for 3 minutes. This is the basic thick white sauce for any soufflé mixture.

Allow the sauce to cool, then beat in the pulp, made from sieved fresh tomatoes, and the canned purée to strengthen the flavour.

Beat the egg yolks thoroughly with the yoghurt and beat into the sauce with a wooden spoon. Season with salt and pepper and dried basil.

Beat the egg whites until they are dry and stiff and, using a metal spoon, fold them into the tomato mixture until they are thoroughly blended.

Turn the mixture into the prepared soufflé dish and stand on a baking sheet. Bake in the centre of the oven at 190°C(375°F)/Gas 5 (solid fuel, 180°C(350°F)) for 45 minutes until risen and golden brown. Serve the soufflé at once, because it recedes very quickly.

You will need a 1-litre (2-pint) soufflé dish. To prepare it, rub the inside with a halved clove of garlic and brush liberally with olive oil. Brush a 'collar' of greaseproof paper to stand about 5 cm (2 ins) above the rim of the dish, wrap it round and fix in place with sticky tape. Remove the paper collar before serving.
*Serves 4*


## Rice Soufflé

Made with cooked, white fish lifted high into the air by four eggs, this soufflé has the effect of a creamy fish sauce served with rice – but it is all baked in one dish.

*1 litre (2 pints) fish stock (made with fish trimmings and herbs)*
*225 g (8 oz) short-grained or 'pudding' rice*
*100 g (4 oz) butter*
*225 g (8 oz) white fish fillet, cooked, skinned and flaked*
*1 small wineglass dry white wine or dry 'cooking' sherry*
*dash red pepper sauce*
*50 g (2 oz) Parmesan cheese, grated*
*150 ml (5 fl oz) natural yoghurt*
*4 eggs, separated*
*salt*
*freshly-ground white pepper*
*cayenne pepper to garnish*

Bring the fish stock to the boil in a large pan, add the rice, cover, bring to the boil and cook for about 10 minutes until the rice is just tender, then strain. Reserve the stock for another use, fish soup, perhaps.

Melt the butter in a large pan and add the fish, wine and pepper sauce. Allow to 'sweat' over a medium heat for about 3 minutes, then stir in the cheese, yoghurt and drained rice and allow to cool. Beat in the egg yolks one at a time and season with salt and pepper. Stiffly whisk the egg whites and gently fold them into the rice mixture with a metal spoon.

Turn into a well-buttered 1-litre (2-pint) soufflé dish and bake at 190°C (375°F)/Gas 5, (solid fuel, 180°C(350°F)) for 20–25 minutes until the soufflé is

well risen and golden brown on top. Sprinkle with cayenne pepper and serve immediately with a green vegetable such as broccoli or French beans, or a fresh green salad.
*Serves 4*

## Flushed Eggs
Aubergines and tomatoes make a rich bed for lightly-poached eggs. Serve with a simple green salad and lemon dressing.

*2 tablespoons olive oil*
*2 large tomatoes, skinned and halved*
*450 g (1 lb) aubergines, diced*
*150 ml (5 fl oz) natural yoghurt*
*4 eggs, lightly poached*
*1 tablespoon fresh chopped parsley to garnish*

For tomato sauce
*1 tablespoon oil*
*1 medium-sized onion, skinned and chopped*
*1 red pepper, trimmed and chopped*
*225 g (8 oz) tomatoes, skinned and chopped*
*1 clove garlic, peeled and crushed*
*salt*
*freshly-ground black pepper*

Heat the oil in a pan and add the tomatoes and diced aubergine. Fry for 5–6 minutes over a moderate heat, stirring carefully without breaking the tomatoes. Stir in the yoghurt and heat gently. Spread the vegetable mixture over the base of a shallow baking dish. Arrange a poached egg on top of each tomato half, cover with tomato sauce and sprinkle with parsley to garnish.

To make the tomato sauce, heat the oil in the original pan and cook the onion, red pepper and tomatoes over a medium heat for 5–6 minutes. Add the garlic and season well. Simmer for a few minutes, stirring, until a smooth paste forms.
*Serves 4*

## Kugel Ring
Noodles baked in a ring mould make an unusual presentation for cooked meat served in a spicy sauce or, cold, for a colourful pepper salad.

*100 g (4 oz) short-cut noodles*
*50 g (2 oz) butter*
*150-ml (¹/₄-pint) carton fresh soured cream*
*225 g (8 oz) yoghurt cheese (see page 5)*
*25 g (1 oz) Parmesan cheese, grated*
*salt*

*freshly-ground black pepper*
*pinch nutmeg*
*2 eggs, beaten*

Cook the noodles in plenty of boiling, salted water until just tender, then drain them well. Melt the butter in a pan and add the warm noodles. Blend together the soured cream, yoghurt cheese and grated Parmesan cheese and stir in the buttered noodles. Season well with salt and pepper and a pinch of nutmeg and bind with the beaten eggs.

Oil a 600-ml (1-pint) ring mould and pack in the noodle mixture. Cover with foil and stand on a baking sheet. Bake at 190°C(375°F)/Gas 5 for 45 minutes, until the mixture is set. Run a sharp knife round the edges of the mould and turn out on to a warm serving dish.

To serve hot, fill with cooked poultry, meat or fish stirred into a white sauce sharpened with curry powder. For a cold dish, prepare a crisp salad of perhaps chicory, red and green peppers and diced cucumber and pile it in the centre.
*Serves 4*


**Stuffed Vine Leaves**
Dolmades, one of the national dishes of Greece, are little parcels of rice plus, wrapped in vine leaves. They can be rice plus meat, plus vegetables, cheese, dried fruit, a handful of herbs, as you will. And they can be served hot or cold, as a main dish, starter or appetizer with drinks.

*4 tablespoons olive oil*
*1 medium-sized onion, skinned and grated*
*1 clove garlic, peeled and crushed*
*1 small aubergine, finely chopped*
*2 tablespoons fresh chopped mint*
*juice of 1/2 lemon*
*175 g (6 oz) long-grain rice*
*600 ml (1 pint) whey (see page 5) or water, boiling*
*salt*
*freshly-ground black pepper*
*12 vine leaves*
*150 g (5 fl oz) natural yoghurt, chilled*
*lemon wedges to serve*

Heat the oil in a large pan and add the onion and garlic. Stir over a moderate heat for 2–3 minutes, then add the aubergine, mint, strained lemon juice, uncooked rice and water or whey, and season well with salt and pepper. Stir well, cover and simmer gently for about 35 minutes until all the liquid has been absorbed.

If using fresh vine leaves, blanch them for just 1 minute in boiling water and pat dry with kitchen paper. Rinse bottled or canned vine leaves in cold water and

dry carefully. Spoon some rice mixture on to the centre of each leaf, wrap up like a tight little parcel and place, joined sides down, in a baking dish. Pour in a little cold water almost to cover the dolmades. Cover with a lid or foil and bake at 180°C(350°F)/Gas 4 for 30 minutes. Drain the dolmades and pat dry. Serve with chilled yoghurt spooned over, and lemon wedges.
*Serves 4*

## Cabbage Parcels
The most basic of ingredients, cabbage and minced meat, can make a dish of high quality.

*1 large white cabbage*
*50 g (2 oz) long-grain rice*
*100 g (4 oz) butter*
*1 large onion, skinned and chopped*
*350 g (12 oz) minced veal*
*salt*
*freshly-ground black pepper*
*1 1/2 teaspoons dill seed*
*1 tablespoon fresh chopped parsley*
*2 egg yolks*
*300 ml (10 fl oz) natural yoghurt*
*50 g (2 oz) Parmesan cheese, grated*

Trim the cabbage of the tough, stubby stalk and cook it whole, in a large pan of boiling, salted water, for 10–12 minutes. Remove the cabbage and pull off the leaves, one at a time. Return the cabbage to the boiling water for a few minutes if the inner leaves do not easily pull away. Pour away the water and reserve the small inner leaves, the 'heart', for another dish.

Cook the rice in boiling, salted water for about 9–10 minutes until it is just tender. Strain the rice and refresh it in cold running water.

Heat half the butter in a frying pan and fry the onion over a medium heat for 4–5 minutes, then add the minced meat and fry, stirring occasionally, until it is lightly browned. Remove the pan from the heat and stir in the rice, salt, pepper, 1 teaspoon of the dill seed and the chopped parsley. Mix well.

Put the cabbage leaves on a large pastry board. Chop off the tough lower stalk of each leaf and discard. Divide the meat mixture between the cabbage leaves and roll them up into separate parcels, completely enclosing the filling.

Melt the remaining butter in the pan and fry the cabbage parcels over moderate heat, a few at a time, to brown them lightly on both sides.

Transfer the rolls to a shallow ovenproof dish, arranging them neatly with the joined sides underneath.

Beat the egg yolks into the yoghurt, season well with salt and pepper and stir in the grated cheese. Pour the sauce over the cabbage rolls and bake in the oven at

180°C(350°F)/Gas 4 for 25–30 minutes until the sauce is golden brown. Serve very hot, sprinkled with the remaining dill seeds. Buttered noodles are a good accompaniment.
*Serves 4*

## Turkish Meat Balls
I once served this dish to local friends for a Boxing Day dinner party, with the remark, 'I hope you don't mind; it's Turkish.' The wife of a poultry farmer, who had just plucked over 400 turkeys for the Christmas trade, thought I said 'turkey' and had to be restrained from leaving the table!

*450 g (1 lb) beef, finely minced 2 or 3 times*
*3 sliced white bread, crusts removed*
*3 eggs*
*1 teaspoon olive oil*
*1 small onion, skinned and grated*
*1 heaped teaspoon fresh chopped parsley*
*1 teaspoon dill seed*
*1 teaspoon fresh chopped dill leaves*
*grated zest of ¹/₂ lemon*
*salt*
*freshly-ground black pepper*
*flour for dusting*
*50 g (2 oz) butter*

For sauce
*3 egg yolks*
*juice of 1 ¹/₂ lemons*
*1 tablespoon water*
*300 ml (10 fl oz) natural yoghurt*

Put the minced meat into a large mixing bowl and pound it thoroughly with the back of a spoon or with a pestle. The success of this dish depends on working the meat to a smooth paste. Soak the crumbled bread in a little water for a few minutes, squeeze it dry and add it to the meat in the bowl. Beat in 2 eggs, the olive oil, grated onion, chopped parsley, dill seed and leaves. Stir in the lemon zest and season well with salt and pepper. The mixture should now be a firm paste. If necessary, knead it to make it smooth.

Rinse your hands in water and form the meat mixture into small balls, not much larger than walnuts.

Bring some salted water to the boil in a frying pan, lower in the meat balls, using a draining spoon, and cover the pan. Poach the meat balls at simmering point for about 15–20 minutes, until they are firm. Remove them from the pan with the draining spoon and allow them to cool.

Beat the third egg and dip the meat balls into it. Roll them in flour, to cover.

108

Melt the butter in the cleaned frying pan and fry the meat balls, turning them over several times, until they are crisp and light brown.

Meanwhile make the sauce. Beat the egg yolks, lemon juice and water in a small bowl. Stir it over a pan of hot water, taking care not to let the water boil. As the sauce thickens, gradually add the yoghurt. Stir until the sauce coats the back of the spoon. Season the sauce with salt and pepper.

Just before serving, pour the sauce into a casserole and gently lower in the meat balls. Serve them with plain boiled rice.
*Serves 4–6*

## Vegetable and Meat Balls
The subtle lemon flavour of these meat balls comes from within, and from the sauce in which they are simmered.

*1 kg (2 lb) leeks, washed and trimmed*
*450 g (1 lb) beef, finely minced 2 or 3 times*
*75 g (3 oz) fresh white breadcrumbs*
*1 egg, beaten*
*120 ml (4 fl oz) natural yoghurt*
*grated zest of ½ lemon*
*salt*
*freshly-ground black pepper*
*oil for frying*

For sauce
*25 g (1 oz) butter*
*juice of 2 lemons*
*240 ml (8 fl oz) water*

Cook the leeks in boiling, salted water for 5–6 minutes, according to size, until they are just tender. Drain them thoroughly and finely chop them. Put the meat in a large mixing bowl and grind it to a smooth paste with a pestle or the back of a spoon. Add the leeks and blend these into the paste. Stir in the breadcrumbs, beaten egg, yoghurt and lemon zest and season well with salt and pepper. Rinse your hands in water and shape the paste into small balls about the size of walnuts. Heat some oil in a pan and shallow-fry the meat balls, turning them occasionally, until they are golden brown. Remove them with a draining spoon, ready to finish cooking them in the sauce.

To make the sauce, put the butter, lemon juice and water into a pan, heat until the butter melts, then add the meat balls and cover the pan. Simmer over a low heat for about 15 minutes, shaking the pan occasionally, until the meat balls have absorbed the sauce.

Serve the meat balls with rice boiled in salted water to which a little lemon juice has been added.
*Serves 6*

## Tandoori Chicken

Tandoori-style cooking is now so popular that there are specialist restaurants in both Britain and America. Although we cannot hope to emulate the flavour obtained by cooking the meat in the traditional clay vessel, we can come close to it with a chicken brick. Failing that, a casserole tightly enclosed with foil under the lid is the next best thing.

*1.25-kg (2¹/₂-lb) chicken, cut into quarters and skinned*
*1 teaspoon salt*
*1 teaspoon garam masala*
*1 teaspoon ground turmeric*
*1 teaspoon ground ginger*
*¹/₂ teaspoon ground cumin seed*
*¹/₂ teaspoon chilli powder*
*2 cloves garlic, peeled and crushed*
*2 bayleaves, crumbled*
*1 tablespoon tomato purée*
*juice of ¹/₂ lemon*
*450 ml (15 fl oz) natural yoghurt*
*100 g (4 oz) ghee (clarified butter)*
*paprika pepper*
*1 lemon, quartered, to garnish*

Pat the chicken dry with kitchen paper. Mix together all the spices with the bayleaves, tomato purée and strained lemon juice, then stir in the yoghurt. Pour half the mixture into a shallow dish, arrange the chicken pieces cut side down and pour the remaining marinade over. Leave to infuse for at least 2 hours – the longer, the better.

Line a chicken brick or casserole dish with greased greaseproof paper or foil. Pour in half the clarified butter. Remove the chicken from the marinade, drain off excess liquid and put the chicken in the dish. Reserve the marinade. Pour on the remaining ghee and tightly close the foil over the chicken. Cover with the lid and cook at 200°C(400°F)/Gas 6 for 1 hour. Open the foil and rub paprika powder well into the chicken flesh. Dry the chicken by returning it to the oven, uncovered, for a further 15 minutes.

Arrange the chicken pieces on a serving dish, garnished with lemon quarters. Heat the marinade and serve separately – it is very hot and spicy. Serve with plain, boiled rice.
*Serves 4*


## Tandoori Fish

I was so pleased with the results from cooking in my earthenware chicken brick that I bought a fish brick, too – and this was the first recipe I tried in it. To achieve the depth of flavour required for this dish it is essential to seal in the fish and

110

spiced sauce so that it cooks in the steam. Without a clay brick, wrap the fish in foil to seal completely.

*1-kg (2-lb) piece of cod*
*3 tablespoons coriander seed*
*8 cardamom seeds*
*2 teaspoons cumin seed*
*8 peppercorns*
*2 teaspoons ground paprika*
*1 teaspoon salt*
*2 tablespoons fresh chopped mint*
*1 medium-sized onion, skinned and finely chopped*
*4 cloves garlic, peeled and crushed*
*300 ml (10 fl oz) natural yoghurt*
*juice of 1 lemon*

Wash the fish, slit it and remove the bone. Pat it dry inside and out with kitchen paper.

Put all the spices and seasonings into a mortar or a large bowl and grind to a paste with the mint, onion and garlic. Stir in the yoghurt and strained lemon juice and mix well. Brush the inside of the fish with the paste. Cut slits in the outside and brush the paste in thoroughly. Pour over any remaining paste and leave the fish to marinate overnight, turning it once or twice if convenient.

Line the fish brick with greased greaseproof paper or foil and lower in the fish. Seal the top to enclose the fish completely, cover with the lid and cook at 180°C(350°F)/Gas 4 for ³/₄–1 hour. The fish should be moist and tender inside and crispy on the outside.

Serve with Cucumber Raita (see page 114) and boiled rice. Colourful side dishes of onion and green pepper rings and lime pickle are attractive accompaniments.
*Serves 4–6*


## Baked Fish with Spiced Sauce
This dish is quickly and easily prepared, yet looks and tastes impressive.

*1 kg (2 lb) white fish fillets, skinned – cod, haddock or coley*
*salt*
*white wine vinegar*
*few pinches chilli powder*
*6 tablespoons ghee (clarified butter)*
*2.5-cm (1-in) length green ginger, scraped*
*1 small onion, skinned and finely chopped*
*2 cloves garlic, peeled and crushed*
*2 teaspoons coriander seed*
*1 teaspoon fennel seed*

111

1 teaspoon cumin seed
1 teaspoon ground turmeric
300 ml (10 fl oz) natural yoghurt
1 lemon, quartered, to serve

Sprinkle the fish fillets with salt, vinegar and a pinch of chilli powder and roll them up, securing each one with a wooden cocktail stick or toothpick. Line a casserole dish with foil, pour in 2 tablespoons of the ghee and arrange the rolled fish. Pour over 2 more tablespoons of ghee, seal the foil over the fish and cover with the lid. Bake at 180°C(350°F)/Gas 4 for 30 minutes.

To make the sauce, chop the ginger finely and put it in a mortar or bowl with the onion, garlic and spices. Grind them to a paste. Heat the remaining ghee in a small pan, add the paste and cook over a low heat for 3–4 minutes. Remove the pan from the heat and beat in the yoghurt. Heat gently without allowing the sauce to boil.

Carefully remove the cooked fish to a heated serving dish and pour a little of the sauce over it. Garnish with the lemon wedges and hand the rest of the sauce separately. Serve with plain boiled rice and poppadoms.
*Serves 4–6*

## Curried Turkey Salad
Cold turkey doesn't seem like just left-overs when it is presented attractively.

300 ml (10 fl oz) natural yoghurt
2 stalks celery, washed and chopped
2 spring onions, trimmed and sliced
1 green pepper, trimmed and chopped
1 tablespoon curry paste
1/2 teaspoon salt
450 g (1 lb) cooked turkey, diced
50 g (2 oz) walnuts, chopped
50 g (2 oz) sultanas
1 lettuce, washed and shredded
1 medium-sized onion, skinned and cut into rings
1 tablespoon fresh chopped chives

Put the yoghurt in a bowl and whip it well. Stir in the prepared celery, spring onions and pepper, then the curry paste and salt. Mix well, then stir in the diced turkey and the walnuts and sultanas. Leave in the refrigerator in a covered container, to chill.

To serve, arrange the shredded lettuce to cover a serving dish and pile the turkey salad into the centre. Arrange the onion rings in a ring around the edge and sprinkle the turkey with the chives. Serve with spiced poppadoms.
*Serves 4*

## Curried Turkey

Yoghurt is the essential ingredient here, the one which blends and mellows all the spices.

*150 ml (5 fl oz) natural yoghurt*
*juice of ¹/₂ lemon*
*4 turkey portions, wings or thighs, skinned and pricked with a darning*
*needle*
*50 g (2 oz) butter*
*1 tablespoon oil*
*3 onions, skinned and sliced*
*3 cloves garlic, peeled and chopped*
*2.5-cm (1-in) length green ginger, scraped and finely chopped*
*1 teaspoon ground turmeric*
*1 teaspoon ground coriander*
*1 teaspoon garam masala*
*1 teaspoon paprika pepper*
*¹/₂ teaspoon ground cumin seed*
*¹/₂ teaspoon chilli powder*
*350 g (12 oz) tomatoes, skinned and chopped*
*salt*
*pinch salt*
*150 ml (¹/₄ pint) whey (see page 5) or stock*

Stir 1 tablespoon of the yoghurt into the strained lemon juice, pour into a shallow dish and marinate the turkey joints for 1 hour, turning them once.

Melt the butter and oil in a flameproof casserole and fry the onion, garlic and ginger over a moderate heat for 5–6 minutes, until the onion is just beginning to colour. Shake the spices together in a bag, sprinkle them into the pan, stir well and cook for 1 minute. Add the turkey portions and cook for 6–8 minutes, turning them so that they brown all over. Add the tomatoes, salt, sugar and liquid, stir well, cover and cook at 150°C(300°F)/Gas 2 for 2 hours. Check the dish during this time and stir in a little more liquid if necessary.

Remove the turkey portions to a heated serving dish. Taste the sauce and add more salt and sugar if needed. If the sauce should be too thin, fast-boil it in the uncovered dish for a few minutes. Stir in the remaining yoghurt, heat gently, and pour the sauce over the meat.

To complete the meal, serve with Vegetable Dhal (see next recipe), Raita (page 114) and Honey Bread (page 51).
*Serves 4*

## Vegetable Dhal

The smooth texture of dhal, a thick lentil purée, makes a good basis for the addition of crisp, slightly crunchy vegetables. You could serve this with rice, a green salad and hot fresh bread as a lunch or supper dish.

*225 g (8 oz) red lentils, soaked overnight*
*500 ml (1 pint) water*
*1 medium-sized onion, skinned and chopped*
*1 large clove garlic, peeled and crushed*
*1/2 teaspoon ground ginger*
*1 teaspoon ground turmeric*
*salt*
*2 tablespoons olive or vegetable oil*
*1 large onion, skinned and chopped*
*2 small courgettes, washed, trimmed and sliced*
*2 teaspoons garam masala*
*1 small cauliflower, boiled until barely tender*
*225 g (8 oz) runner beans, broken into 2.5-cm (1-in) strips and boiled*
*    until barely tender*
*3 large tomatoes, skinned and chopped*

Discard any lentils that are discoloured and those that float to the top. Cook the lentils in the water with the medium-sized onion, garlic, ginger and turmeric until the lentils have absorbed the water and are tender – about $1/2$–$3/4$ of an hour. Remove from the heat, add salt and beat with a wooden spoon.

Meanwhile heat the oil in a frying pan, add the large onion, the sliced courgettes and the garam masala and fry, stirring gently, until the onion is just soft. Drain the partly-cooked cauliflower and beans. Break up the cauliflower into small florets, add the vegetables to the frying pan with the tomatoes, and heat through.

Mix all the vegetables into the dhal, stirring carefully to avoid breaking them up.
*Serves 4*


## Cucumber Raita

A cool, refreshing salad to serve as an accompaniment to curry.

*1/2 cucumber, washed and peeled*
*salt*
*150 ml (5 fl oz) natural yoghurt, chilled*
*freshly-ground black pepper*
*juice of 1/2 lemon*

Grate the cucumber on a medium grater. Sprinkle with salt and set aside for 30 minutes. Press the cucumber gently to remove excess liquid and pat it dry with a piece of crumpled-up kitchen paper. Fold the cucumber into the yoghurt, season well and add the lemon juice; stir well to blend. Serve chilled.
*Serves 4*

## Cauliflower and Bean Curry

Vegetable curries may be served as the main dish of a vegetarian meal, with crisp accompaniments, or as a complement to baked meat or fish dishes.

*2 tablespoons ghee (clarified butter)*
*1 medium-sized onion, skinned and sliced*
*2 cloves garlic, peeled and crushed*
*1 teaspoon ground turmeric*
*1 teaspoon ground coriander*
*1/2 teaspoon freshly-ground black pepper*
*4 cloves, crushed*
*1/2 teaspoon chilli powder*
*350 g (12 oz) runner beans, trimmed and cut into 3.5-cm (1 1/2-in) lengths*
*1 small cauliflower, washed and cut into florets*
*300 ml (10 fl oz) natural yoghurt*
*1/2 teaspoon salt*
*juice of 1 lemon*
*desiccated coconut, toasted, to garnish (optional)*

Heat the ghee in a pan and fry the onion and garlic over a moderate heat for 5–6 minutes until the onion turns light brown. Add all the spices and fry, stirring, for 2 minutes. Add the prepared vegetables and yoghurt and season with salt and the strained lemon juice. Blend well, cover the pan and simmer over a low heat for 35–40 minutes until the vegetables are tender. Serve in a heated casserole, garnished, if you like, with toasted desiccated coconut.
*Serves 4*

## Paprika Potatoes

It sometimes makes a pleasant change to serve a spiced vegetable dish with plain meat or fish. Or if your love of spices knows no bounds, with a dish already scented with paprika.

*1 kg (2 lb) potatoes, peeled*
*40 g (1 1/2 oz) butter*
*1 medium-sized onion, skinned and finely chopped*
*2 cloves garlic, peeled and finely chopped*
*1 tablespoon paprika pepper*
*1/4 teaspoon caraway seeds*
*1 large tomato, skinned and chopped*
*1 green pepper, trimmed and diced*
*450 ml (3/4 pint) chicken stock*
*salt*
*freshly-ground black pepper*
*150 ml (5 fl oz) natural yoghurt*
*1 tablespoon fresh chopped chives to garnish*

Cook the potatoes in boiling, salted water for 7–8 minutes, until they are barely tender. Drain them and cut them into 1-cm (½-in) slices. Melt the butter in a pan and fry the onion and garlic over a medium heat for 4–5 minutes. Stir in the paprika pepper and caraway seeds and add the chopped tomato, green pepper and potatoes. Pour on the chicken stock, stir well and season with salt and pepper. Bring to the boil and simmer gently for 20 minutes. Stir in the yoghurt and reheat without boiling. Serve sprinkled with the chopped chives.
*Serves 4–6*

## Cream of Onions
A smooth way to serve onions, especially good with roast lamb.

>675 g (1½ lb) onions, skinned
>150 ml (5 fl oz) natural yoghurt
>100 g (4 oz) yoghurt cheese (see page 5)
>salt
>freshly-ground black pepper
>15 g (½ oz) butter
>2 tablespoons fresh breadcrumbs
>2 eggs, hard boiled and shelled

Put the whole onions in a pan of boiling, salted water and boil for 15–20 minutes, until they are tender. Drain them well and slice them. Arrange the onions in the base of a greased pie dish and keep them warm. Mix together the yoghurt and yoghurt cheese, heat it gently in a small pan, beat well and season with salt and pepper. Pour this over the onions. Melt the butter in the same pan and fry the breadcrumbs until they are dry and crisp. Stir in the chopped hard-boiled eggs and sprinkle over the dish. Serve hot.
*Serves 4*

## Creamed Haricot Beans
A lovely way to combine two fresh spring vegetables.

>225 g (8 oz) fresh haricot beans (shelled weight)
>4 small carrots, peeled or scraped and thickly sliced
>15 g (½ oz) butter

>For sauce
>25 g (1 oz) butter
>25 g (1 oz) flour
>300 ml (½ pint) chicken stock (or use water and stock cube), hot
>salt
>freshly-ground black pepper
>1 egg yolk
>75 ml (2½ fl oz) natural yoghurt
>1 tablespoon fresh chopped basil or parsley

116

Cook the shelled beans in boiling, salted water for 10–12 minutes, until they are just tender, and drain them. In another pan, cook the carrots in boiling, salted water for about 15 minutes – depending on size – and drain them. Put the butter in a heated ovenproof dish, add and toss the beans and carrots and keep them warm.

To make the sauce, melt the butter in a pan, stir in the flour and cook for 1 minute over a moderate heat. Gradually pour on the stock, stirring, and bring to the boil. Season well with salt and pepper and simmer for 3 minutes, stirring. Beat together the egg yolk and yoghurt, pour in a little of the sauce, then add the egg mixture to the sauce in the pan. Stir in the fresh herb and heat the sauce gently, without allowing it to boil. Pour the sauce over the vegetables and stir gently with a wooden spoon to blend the butter into the sauce.
*Serves 4*

## Beetroot in Yoghurt Sauce
There's such a richness about the colour of cooked beetroot, and such a fantastic contrast with the pale creaminess of the yoghurt – it just *has* to taste good.

*450 g (1 lb) small beetroot*

*For sauce*
*15 g (¹/₂ oz) butter*
*1 medium-sized onion, skinned and grated*
*3 cloves garlic, peeled and crushed*
*grated zest of ¹/₂ lemon*
*300 ml (10 fl oz) natural yoghurt*
*salt*
*freshly-ground black pepper*
*1 dessertspoon fresh chopped parsley*

Twist the leaves from the beetroot about 2.5 cm (1 in) from the top of the vegetable. (Do not cut them off, as this causes more 'bleeding' and loss of colour.) Wash the beetroot and cook them in boiling, salted water for 30–45 minutes, depending on age and size. Drain them, refresh in cold running water and skin them. Put the beetroot in a heated serving dish and keep them warm.

To make the sauce, melt the butter in a small pan and gently fry the onion and garlic until it is soft. Remove the pan from the heat and stir in the lemon rind. Beat in the yoghurt, season with salt and pepper and when the mixture is smooth, return the pan to a low heat until the sauce is hot. Stir occasionally and do not allow it to boil. Pour the sauce over the beetroot just before serving. Sprinkle with the parsley.
*Serves 4–6*

CHAPTER SEVEN

# *Delicate, Delicious Puddings*

It is impossible to exaggerate the importance of the pudding course. At banquets, the dessert has for centuries been the *pièce de resistance* of the meal, the chef's opportunity to show off his flair for presentation and showmanship, and send to the table a pudding flaming in brandy, a massive moulded confection with layers of ice-cold surprise ingredients, or a pastry created with all the structural detail of a piece of architecture.

At home, of course, we do not aspire to these heights, but we nevertheless want to send our guests away with the impression of a course lovingly prepared, and in perfect harmony with the rest of the meal.

I am sometimes asked to help with the cooking for the various fund-raising supper parties we hold in the village, and I can't help thinking that the most popular event of all would be a pudding party. No matter how good a selection of hot or cold dishes we offer for the main course, it is the pudding table that attracts the queues. Guests who have politely refused second helpings of the casserole on the grounds that they are full up will feel it their duty to pile a spoonful of mousse on top of a slice of pie, or take a fruit fool to follow the cheesecake. And then come back for more.

And it is in this course, in the preparation of puddings, that I have found yoghurt most indispensable. Few of us can afford the cash or the calories that lashings of heavy cream cost us, and so I have been substituting natural yoghurt in place of all or part of the cream called for in some of my favourite recipes. When an ice-cream with no cream at all turned out perfectly and didn't crystallize, I knew the whole chapter was going to be a doddle. Try it. Follow these

118

recipes if you will, but please try making some of your own favourites with yoghurt. You will find them just as delicious and a good deal more delicate.

## Yoghurt Cream of Creams

*Coeur à la crème* is a classic summer accompaniment to soft berry fruits, so rich that, to slimmers, it seems positively sinful. This one, with cottage cheese and yoghurt, tastes good and is less fattening.

>    *350 g (12 oz) cottage cheese*
>    *150 ml (5 fl oz) natural yoghurt, chilled*
>    *2 tablespoons water*
>    *2 teaspoons powdered gelatine*

Sieve the cottage cheese into a bowl and beat in the yoghurt. Pour the water into a cup and sprinkle on the gelatine. Stand the cup in a small bowl of hot water and stir until the gelatine dissolves. Pour the gelatine into the cheese mixture and blend well. Spoon the mixture into four individual moulds or cocotte dishes, cover them with muslin and secure with rubber bands or string. Stand the containers upside down on a wire rack over a dish and leave to drain in the refrigerator overnight. Turn out the moulds and serve, chilled, with fresh or thawed frozen strawberries, raspberries or blackberries, or with Swaying Fruit (see next recipe).
*Serves 4*

## Swaying Fruit

Why swaying fruit? Because the fruit juice is thickened so slightly that it isn't set hard, like a jelly. It just sways!

>    *225 g (8 oz) redcurrants*
>    *225 g (8 oz) raspberries* or *loganberries*
>    *225 g (8 oz) blackcurrants*
>    *2 tablespoons water*
>    *225 g (8 oz) caster sugar*
>    *arrowroot, in the proportion of 15 g (½ oz) to each 600 ml (1 pint) fruit juice*
>    *150 ml (5 fl oz) natural yoghurt, chilled*

Wash and stem the fruit, put it in a pan with the water and cook until the fruit is soft. Rub it through a sieve and measure the juice. Return the fruit juice to the cleaned pan, add the sugar and bring slowly to the boil, stirring occasionally until the sugar dissolves.

Blend the arrowroot with a little water to make a smooth paste and gradually pour into the fruit juice, stirring. Bring the mixture to the boil and simmer for 2 minutes, until the cloudiness clears.

Pour into 4 individual serving bowls and allow to cool. Top with a swirl of whipped yoghurt and serve well chilled.

Shortbread fans (see next recipe) are delicious with this rather slender dessert.
*Serves 4*


## Shortbread Fans
Home-made biscuits are always more special than bought ones. They keep well in a tin, so need not take time to make when you're busy.

*50 g (2 oz) caster sugar*
*100 g (4 oz) plain flour*
*50 g (2 oz) self-raising flour*
*25 g (1 oz) cornflour*
*150 g (5 oz) unsalted butter, softened*
*¹/₄ teaspoon vanilla essence*
*extra caster sugar to dust*

Lightly flour a baking sheet.

Sift the sugar and flours into a bowl and rub in the butter. Add the vanilla essence and knead the mixture until it forms a firm dough. Roll out on a lightly-floured board to a thickness of about 0.5 cm (¹/₄ in). Using a plate as a guide, cut out three circles about 18 cm (7 ins) in diameter. Mark each one lightly into eight segments. Sprinkle the circles with a little caster sugar. Bake each one on a baking sheet at 170°C(325°F)/Gas 3 for 15–20 minutes, until lightly browned. Leave the shortbread on the baking sheet for 5 minutes to cool before transferring on to a wire rack. When cool break into segments and put the biscuits into an airtight container.
*Makes 24 biscuits*


## Raspberry Syllabub
One of the delights of summer – raspberries and cream prepared in this traditional way.

*350 g (12 oz) fresh raspberries, or frozen ones, thawed*
*75 g (3 oz) caster sugar*
*¹/₂ teaspoon grated lemon rind*
*2 tablespoons lemon juice*
*150 ml (5 fl oz) natural yoghurt, chilled*
*300 ml (¹/₂ pint) double cream, whipped*
*300 ml (¹/₂ pint) sweet white wine*

Reserve a few of the biggest raspberries to decorate. Put the remainder into a bowl, add half the sugar, the lemon rind and lemon juice and mash well with a wooden spoon until the fruit is pulped.

120

Add the yoghurt to the whipped cream and beat until the mixture is stiff, then gradually beat in the wine and remaining sugar. If this is done carefully, the cream mixture will take up the wine without separating.

Fold the cream mixture into the raspberry pulp and stir with a metal spoon until it is well blended.

Spoon the syllabub into 4 or 6 tall glasses or goblets and decorate with the reserved raspberries. Serve well chilled, with sponge finger biscuits (see next recipe).

*Serves 4–6*

## Sponge Finger Biscuits

Bought sponge fingers are fine, but for times when you want to take pride in the fact that everything on the table is home-made, here's the recipe. The biscuits keep well in a tin.

*6 eggs, separated*
*150 g (5 oz) caster sugar*
*few drops vanilla essence*
*150 g (5 oz) flour, sifted*
*extra caster sugar to dust*

Grease and flour a baking sheet.

Cream together the egg yolks and sugar until light and fluffy, then beat in the vanilla essence. Whisk the egg whites until they are stiff, then fold them into the creamed mixture with the flour.

Fit a large, plain nozzle into a piping bag and pipe strips of the mixture on to the baking sheet, about 5 cm (2 ins) apart. Dust the tops of the fingers lightly with caster sugar and bake at 180°C(350°F)/Gas 4 for 5–6 minutes, until the biscuits are a light golden brown. Allow them to cool on the sheet, then lift them on to a wire rack. When they are completely cold, store them in an airtight container.

*Makes about 45 biscuits*

## Apricot Flummery

A light, whipped concoction, made much lighter because the base is yoghurt and not the usual double cream.

*4 egg yolks*
*75 g (3 oz) caster sugar*
*3 tablespoons apricot liqueur*
*300 ml (10 fl oz) natural yoghurt, whipped (or use apricot-flavoured yoghurt)*

Put the egg yolks and sugar into a basin which fits over a pan of hot – not boiling – water. Beat until the mixture thickens, then gradually pour on the liqueur and continue beating until the mixture stands in stiff peaks. (Needless to say, an electric beater is almost a 'must' for this operation.) Remove the bowl from the heat and allow the mixture to cool.

Fold the whipped yoghurt into the eggs and pour into four tall glasses or goblets. Put in the refrigerator or a cold place to chill before serving.

Decorate each glass with either a few drops of the liqueur, a slice of fresh or canned fruit, or a sponge finger biscuit (see page 121) pushed into the top.
*Serves 4*

## Almond Cream

A taste of almonds in this creamy dessert is enriched by the addition of crushed macaroons.

*150 ml (5 fl oz) natural yoghurt, chilled*
*150 ml (¹/₄ pint) double cream, whipped*
*2 egg whites*
*1 dessertspoon caster sugar*
*100 g (4 oz) almonds, blanched, toasted and roughly chopped*
*50 g (2 oz) macaroon biscuits, crushed*
*pinch salt*
*1 tablespoon sweet Marsala*

Fold the yoghurt into the whipped cream and beat until the mixture is stiff. In another bowl, stiffly whisk the egg whites and, using a metal spoon, carefully fold in the sugar, three-quarters of the toasted almonds, the crushed macaroons and the salt. Stir gently to blend, then fold the egg whites into the cream mixture, with the Marsala.

Spoon into six glasses or individual dishes and sprinkle with the reserved chopped almonds. Chill well before serving.
*Serves 6*

## Golden Honey Fool

When you're low on fresh or frozen fruit, here's a lovely pudding which can be made from the store cupboard.

*175 g (6 oz) dried apricots*
*175 g (6 oz) dried apple rings*
*2 bananas, sliced*
*150 ml (5 fl oz) natural yoghurt, chilled*
*1 tablespoon clear honey*

Soak the dried apricots and apples overnight in cold water. Drain the fruit and put into a blender with the banana slices, yoghurt and honey. Blend for 1–2 minutes. Without a blender, sieve the apricots, apples and bananas into a bowl, add the yoghurt and honey and whisk. Pour into 4 individual dishes and chill. Serve with shortbread fans (see page 120).
*Serves 4*

## Mango Mousse
Capture the flavour of the Caribbean with this mousse made from thick, syrupy canned mango juice.

*3 eggs, separated*
*50 g (2 oz) caster sugar*
*300 ml (1/2 pint) canned mango juice*
*15 g (1/2 oz) powdered gelatine*
*150 ml (5 fl oz) natural yoghurt, whipped*

Whisk the egg yolks and sugar together in a bowl over a pan of hot, not boiling, water until the mixture is thick and creamy. Pour a little of the mango juice into a small bowl, sprinkle on the gelatine and stand in hot water. Stir to dissolve the gelatine, then pour in a steady stream into the egg mixture, whisking all the time. Remove the pan from the heat and whisk the mixture until it cools. Whisk in the rest of the mango juice and the yoghurt and leave in the refrigerator or a cold place until the mixture begins to set. Fold in the stiffly-beaten egg whites and pour the mousse into a straight-sided soufflé dish. Leave in the refrigerator or a cold place to set. Decorate the top with slices of fresh or canned fruit or chopped nuts. Serve with sponge finger biscuits (see page 121).
*Serves 6–8*

## Honey Posset
Just occasionally, time might be more precious than money. Here's a dessert that can be whipped up in less time than it takes to clear the plates from the previous course.

*grated rind and juice of 1 lemon*
*300 ml (1/2 pint) double cream*
*300 ml (10 fl oz) natural yoghurt, chilled*
*6 tablespoons clear honey*
*150 ml (1/4 pint) sweet sherry*

Put all the ingredients together in a large bowl and, with an electric beater, if available, beat until the mixture is thick enough to hold the trail of a spoon. Pour the mixture into six glasses or individual dishes and chill. Serve with shortbread fans (see page 120).
*Serves 6*

## Gooseberry Fool
Economize on cash and calories by making fruit fools – using any seasonal, frozen or canned fruits – with half double cream and half natural yoghurt.

*675 g (1 1/2 lb) gooseberries, topped and tailed*
*75 g (3 oz) soft light brown sugar*

*150 ml (5 fl oz) natural yoghurt, chilled*
*150 ml (¹/₄ pint) double cream, whipped*
*50 g (2 oz) plain chocolate, grated*

Put the gooseberries in a pan with very little water, just enough to prevent the fruit from sticking before the juice runs. Cook them over a moderate heat until they are soft, add the sugar and stir until it dissolves. Sieve or liquidize the fruit and allow to cool.

Fold the yoghurt into the whipped cream and whip until the mixture is stiff. Fold the cream mixture into the fruit purée and stir to blend thoroughly.

Spoon the fruit fool into 4 individual bowls and decorate with the grated chocolate. Serve well chilled.
*Serves 4*

### Ginger Ice Cream

Or, more precisely, ginger ice yoghurt, for there's no cream at all in this lovely, smooth rich dessert.

*300 ml (¹/₂ pint) milk*
*2 eggs, separated*
*3 tablespoons ginger syrup*
*4 tablespoons clear honey*
*300 ml (10 fl oz) natural yoghurt, chilled*
*50 g (2 oz) stem ginger, finely chopped*

*For sauce*
*75 ml (1 gill) water*
*2 tablespoons clear honey*
*3 tablespoons ginger syrup*
*1 teaspoon cornflour*
*¹/₂ teaspoon ground ginger*
*3 tablespoons lemon juice*
*75 g (3 oz) stem ginger, finely chopped*

Put the milk and egg yolks in a bowl resting over a pan of hot water and stir the mixture over a very low heat – the water must not boil. When the custard starts to thicken, remove it from the heat, stir in the ginger syrup and honey and leave to cool. Pour into a chilled container, cover and freeze at lowest temperature setting for 1 hour, until the sides are frozen but the centre is still soft. Turn the mixture out into a chilled bowl and beat until smooth. Whisk the egg whites until they form peaks and fold them and the yoghurt into the custard. Stir in the chopped ginger. Return to the freezer for 3–4 hours, until firm. Allow the ice cream to thaw in the refrigerator for 1 hour before serving.

To make the sauce, put the water, honey and ginger syrup into a pan over a moderate heat. Put the cornflour and ground ginger into a small bowl and pour on the lemon juice, stirring to blend well. Add to the sauce in the pan, bring to the boil and boil for 3 minutes, stirring. Add the chopped ginger, pour into a jug and leave to cool.

To serve, spoon the ice cream into a dish, pour over a little of the sauce and serve the rest separately.
*Serves 6–8*


## Vanilla Ice

With a supply of this basic ice in the freezer, you can make a variety of different sauces to ring the changes.

*450 ml (15 fl oz) natural yoghurt*
*1 vanilla pod, split lengthwise*
*75 g (3 oz) caster sugar*
*120 ml (¹/₅ pint) water*
*4 egg yolks*

Put the yoghurt into a small pan with the split vanilla pod and leave over a very low heat for 5–6 minutes to infuse. Strain and allow the yoghurt to cool. (You can wash and dry the vanilla pod for use another time, though the flavour will be less pronounced.)

Put the sugar and water into a pan over a moderate heat and stir to dissolve the sugar, then bring to the boil and fast-boil for 3–4 minutes until the syrup reaches the thread stage, 112°C(230°F), when a drop of the cooled syrup will form a thread if rubbed between finger and thumb. Dip your fingers first into cold water, then into the syrup, then into water again to test. Allow the syrup to cool slightly. Whisk the egg yolks and gradually pour the syrup on to them, whisking until the mixture is thick. Whip the yoghurt, and fold it in.

Pour the mixture into a chilled container, cover and freeze at the lowest temperature in the freezer or freezing compartment of the refrigerator. Leave for about 1 hour, until the outside of the custard has set. Turn into a chilled bowl and whisk vigorously for 3–4 minutes. Return to the container, cover and freeze for at least 3 hours, stirring once or twice during this time. Thaw for 30 minutes in the refrigerator before serving.

Serve the ice cream with a sauce, mixed with other flavoured ice creams, or plain with shortbread fans (see page 120).
*Serves 6*


## Chocolate Ice Cream

To make chocolate ice cream, follow the basic vanilla recipe, but add 175 g (6 oz) plain chocolate, broken into squares, to the yoghurt and vanilla pod in the saucepan. Serve with lemon or cherry-flavoured yoghurt.

## Chocolate Peppermint Sauce
A sauce with that lovely flavour of after-dinner peppermint creams.

*50 g (2 oz) plain chocolate, broken into squares*
*25 g (1 oz) sugar*
*1 teaspoon cocoa powder*
*1 teaspoon powdered instant coffee*
*300 ml (1/2 pint) water*
*1 teaspoon peppermint essence*
*1 egg yolk*
*2 teaspoons water, warm*
*25 g (1 oz) blanched almonds, toasted and chopped*

Put the broken chocolate, sugar, cocoa powder, coffee powder and water into a pan over low heat, stirring to dissolve the sugar. Increase the heat, bring to the boil and simmer for 10–15 minutes. Stir in the peppermint essence and remove from the heat.

Beat together the egg yolk and warm water, pour on a little of the warm chocolate sauce and pour the mixture into the pan. Mix well and heat gently, without allowing the sauce to boil.

Serve hot over vanilla ice cream, sprinkled with chopped almonds.
*Serves 6*

## Fruit Sauce
To serve with ice cream.

*1 banana*
*2 teaspoons lemon juice*
*2 tablespoons jam – apple, apricot, pineapple or quince*
*2 tablespoons rum (optional)*
*4 tablespoons pineapple syrup (from can)*
*100 g (4 oz) canned pineapple tit-bits*
*25 g (1 oz) green grapes, halved and seeded*
*25 g (1 oz) black grapes, halved and seeded*
*25 g (1 oz) maraschino cherries, quartered*

Peel and slice the banana and sprinkle with the lemon juice. In a small pan heat together the jam, rum if used and pineapple syrup over a moderate heat. Remove the pan from the cooker and stir in the remaining ingredients. Allow to cool.

Pour the cold fruit sauce over vanilla ice cream, and serve with sponge finger biscuits (see page 121).
*Serves 6*

## Yuletide Sauce
When it's the season of Christmas pudding and mince pies, even ice cream can get into the mood with this rich mincemeat sauce.

*225 g (8 oz) mincemeat*
*grated zest and juice of 1 orange*
*4 tablespoons brandy*
*25 g (1 oz) blanched almonds, chopped*

Put the ingredients together in a small pan, stir well with a wooden spoon and leave over a moderate heat for 4–5 minutes to heat through.

Pour the hot sauce over vanilla ice cream, and serve with shortbread fans (see page 120).


## Apricot Ice Cream

Fruit-flavoured yoghurt can be served as an instant sauce with ice creams of similar or complementary flavours. Use this recipe as a basic one, substituting any seasonal or frozen fruit purée you have. Vary the accompanying flavour, too. For example, hazelnut yoghurt is delicious with apricot ice cream; lemon or cherry yoghurt with chocolate ice cream (see page 125), chocolate yoghurt with cherry ice cream (use a purée of canned, stoned cherries to make this).

*75 g (3 oz) caster sugar*
*120 ml (¹/₅ pint) water*
*4 egg yolks*
*450 ml (15 fl oz) natural yoghurt, chilled and whipped*
*450 ml (³/₄ pint) apricot purée (made from fresh, dried or canned apricots)*

For sauce
*2 150-ml (5-fl oz) cartons apricot yoghurt, chilled*

Put the sugar and water into a pan over a moderate heat and stir until the sugar has dissolved. Increase the heat, bring to the boil and boil rapidly for 3–4 minutes until the temperature of the syrup, at 112°C(230°F), reaches the 'thread' stage (see Vanilla Ice recipe, page 125, for method of testing without a sugar thermometer). Take the pan from the heat and allow the syrup to cool slightly.

Whisk the egg yolks and slowly pour on the syrup. Continue whisking until the mixture thickens, then fold in the whipped yoghurt and apricot purée.

Turn the mixture into a chilled container, cover and freeze at the lowest temperature in the freezer or freezing compartment of the refrigerator for about 1 hour, until the edge has set firm. Transfer to a chilled bowl and whisk well for 3–4 minutes. Return to the container, cover and freeze for a further 3–4 hours, until set firm. Allow the ice cream to rest in the refrigerator for 30 minutes before serving.

Serve the ice cream with the apricot yoghurt (or another flavour of your choice) poured over.
*Serves 6*

**Ratafia Ice Cream**

An adaptation of a scrumptious Italian ice cream recipe, now made with half yoghurt and half double cream, that is one of my own dinner party favourites. With a tin of this ice cream in the freezer, there is always an instant, and very good, dessert on hand. It takes only seconds to surround the block with sponge fingers and crumble a few biscuits over the top.

*300 ml (¹/₂ pint) double cream, chilled*
*300 ml (10 fl oz) natural yoghurt, chilled*
*50 g (2 oz) icing sugar, sifted*
*pinch salt*
*100 g (4 oz) ratafia biscuits, crushed*
*1 wineglass Marsala or sweet sherry*
*about 18 sponge finger biscuits, bought or home-made (see page 121)*
*a few maraschino cherries and angelica strips to decorate*

Put the chilled cream and yoghurt into a bowl with the icing sugar and salt and whisk until thick. Pour into a chilled container, cover and freeze at the lowest temperature in the freezer or freezing compartment of the refrigerator for about 1 hour, until a 'crust' has formed on the outside.

Turn the mixture into a chilled bowl, stir in the ratafia biscuit crumbs, reserving 1 tablespoon to decorate, and the wine and beat vigorously. Pour the mixture into a 450-g (1-lb) loaf tin, cover with foil and freeze until firm, about 3 hours. There is no need to stir this ice cream during the freezing period.

Take the ice cream from the freezer about 30 minutes before serving. Turn it out on to an oblong serving dish. Cut the sponge finger biscuits in half and build a wall of them all around the block of ice cream, cut sides at the bottom. The biscuits slope inwards to the top, so will not topple over backwards. Sprinkle the reserved biscuit crumbs over the top and decorate with a bunch of maraschino cherries, with 'stalks' of thin strips of angelica.

**Holly Ice Cream**

Much quicker to make than Christmas pudding, and much lighter, too. A brandy and fruit-flavoured ice cream topped, of course, with a sprig of holly.

*300 ml (¹/₂ pint) milk*
*1 vanilla pod, split lengthwise*
*2 eggs*
*75 g (3 oz) caster sugar*
*100 g (4 oz) mincemeat*
*50 g (2 oz) glacé cherries, washed, dried and quartered*
*2 tablespoons brandy*
*300 ml (10 fl oz) natural yoghurt, chilled and whipped*
*holly or a few glacé cherries and candied angelica to decorate*

In a pan, heat the milk and vanilla. Beat the eggs and sugar together in a bowl, remove the vanilla pod from the pan, then pour on the hot (not boiling) milk. Strain the mixture from the bowl into the cleaned pan and, over a low heat, stir until it thickens into a custard. Remove the pan from the heat and stand in cold water to cool.

Stir the mincemeat, chopped cherries and brandy into the cooled mixture, then fold in the whipped yoghurt.

Turn the mixture into a pudding basin, cover with foil and freeze for 3–4 hours. Remove from the freezer about 30 minutes before serving. Turn the ice cream out on to a serving plate and decorate with a sprig of holly. If no holly is available, use halved glacé cherries for the berries and other evergreen leaves, or strips of candied angelica.
*Serves 8*


## Butterscotch Snowball

The lovely rich, smooth flavour of butterscotch is even nicer when it's frozen.

*25 g (1 oz) butter*
*100 g (4 oz) soft dark brown sugar*
*150 ml (¼ pint) water*
*25 g (1 oz) blanched almonds, ground*
*4 egg yolks*
*25 g (1 oz) caster sugar*
*1 teaspoon vanilla essence*
*300 ml (10 fl oz) yoghurt, chilled and whipped*
*25 g (1 oz) caster sugar to decorate*
*25 g (1 oz) blanched almonds, toasted, to decorate*

Put the butter and sugar into a pan over a moderate heat, and stir until the sugar dissolves. Increase the heat, bring to the boil and boil for 1 minute. Remove from the heat while you gradually pour on the water, stirring well with a wooden spoon. Return the pan to the heat and stir until the butterscotch has dissolved. Stir in the ground almonds and take the pan from the heat.

Whisk together the egg yolks and caster sugar until the mixture is light and creamy, and gradually pour in the butterscotch, beating all the time. Mix in the vanilla essence and leave to cool. Then fold the whipped yoghurt into the mixture. Pour into a chilled container and cover. Put into the freezer or freezing compartment of the refrigerator at the lowest temperature, and freeze for 1 hour, until the mixture is frozen at the edges. Turn into a chilled bowl and whisk well, then return the mixture to a basin, cover and freeze for a further 3–4 hours until it is firm. To prevent ice crystals forming, stir once or twice during the freezing time.

Remove the frozen pudding from the freezer and leave in the refrigerator for 30

minutes before serving. Serve sprinkled with a 'frost' of caster sugar and the toasted almonds.
*Serves 4*

## Orange Mint Sorbet
Fresh oranges and frozen sorbet topped, for extra coolness, with frosted mint sprigs.

> *300 ml (10 fl oz) natural yoghurt, chilled*
> *1 can frozen unsweetened orange juice, thawed*
> *2 oranges*
> *1 tablespoon powdered gelatine*
> *3 tablespoons water*
> *2 egg whites*
> *4 sprigs mint to decorate*
> *caster sugar*

In a bowl, mix together the yoghurt, thawed orange juice and grated zest of the two oranges. Sprinkle the gelatine on the water in a small bowl, stand in hot water and stir to dissolve. Pour into the orange mixture, stir well and leave in the refrigerator or a cold place until it begins to set. Beat the egg whites. Dip the sprigs of mint in egg white, then in caster sugar and leave on a plate to dry. Fold the egg whites into the orange mixture, cover the container and freeze.

Pare the pith from the oranges and cut them in slices. Spoon layers of the sorbet into four tall glasses, alternating with orange slices. Top with sorbet and decorate with the frosted mint sprigs.
*Serves 4*

## Madeira Mould
A decorative mould evocative of the past, with the rich and unmistakable flavour of Madeira.

> *4 eggs, separated*
> *300 ml (10 fl oz) natural yoghurt*
> *50 g (2 oz) caster sugar*
> *15 g (¹/₂ oz) powdered gelatine*
> *3 tablespoons water*
> *3 tablespoons Madeira (or use sweet sherry or Marsala)*
> *40 g (1¹/₂ oz) hazelnuts, toasted*

Put the egg yolks, yoghurt and sugar into a bowl and whisk well. Stand the bowl over a pan of hot, not boiling, water and heat, stirring occasionally until the mixture thickens. Sprinkle the gelatine over the water in a small bowl, stand in hot water and stir to dissolve.

Take the pan from the heat, pour in the dissolved gelatine mixture and the

130

wine and whisk. Put aside until it begins to set. Stiffly beat the egg whites and fold
them carefully into the mixture. Pour into a wetted 750-ml (1½-pint) mould and
leave in a refrigerator or a cold place to set. Turn out the mould on to a serving
dish and decorate with rings of toasted hazelnuts; for an old-time feeling, serve
with slices of Madeira cake.
*Serves 6*


## Pear Cream
Fresh fruit and yoghurt make an instant pudding that's quicker to prepare than
most packaged ones.

*4 dessert pears*
*2 tablespoons lemon juice*
*2 150-ml (5-fl oz) cartons hazelnut yoghurt, chilled*
*ground cinnamon*
*25 g (1 oz) hazelnuts, chopped (reserve 4 to decorate)*

Peel, core and quarter the pears and toss them in the lemon juice to preserve their
colour. Arrange them in a shallow serving bowl and spoon over the hazelnut
yoghurt. Sprinkle with a few pinches of ground cinnamon and then with the
chopped nuts. Decorate with the reserved nuts. Serve, well chilled, with plain
chocolate finger biscuits.
*Serves 4*


## Plum Charlottes
A delicious way to use up a generous over-ordering of bread. It *has* to be at least a
day old for this recipe.

*50 g (2 oz) butter*
*8 0.5-cm (½-in) thick slices bread, cut from a large white loaf*
*25 g (1 oz) soft light brown sugar*
*675 g (1½ lb) plums*
*75 g (3 oz) granulated sugar*
*2 150-ml (5-fl oz) cartons hazelnut yoghurt, chilled*
*4 hazelnuts to decorate*

Melt the butter in a small pan. Grate the bread or put it into a blender to make fine
crumbs. Remove the pan from the heat and stir in the breadcrumbs and brown
sugar. Allow to cool.

Put the plums in a pan with the granulated sugar and very little water. Cover
and cook over a moderate heat until the fruit is soft. Remove the stones and
liquidize or sieve the fruit.

To assemble the pudding, choose four individual sundae dishes or a glass bowl
and make layers of the crumb mixture, the plum purée and the chilled yoghurt,

starting with crumbs and ending with yoghurt. Decorate with the hazelnuts and chill well before serving.
*Serves 4*

## Spring Custards

The pale green, yellow and white stripes of this light pudding look like the very essence of spring. You can vary the fruit base according to the season, or use thick, slightly sweetened fruit purée.

*350 g (12 oz) gooseberries, topped and tailed*
*300 ml (10 fl oz) natural yoghurt*
*2 egg yolks*
*75 g (3 oz) caster sugar*
*1 egg white*

Put the gooseberries into a pan with very little water and cook over a moderate heat until they just begin to soften. Divide them between 4 cocotte dishes. Beat the yoghurt and egg yolks together with one-third of the sugar and pour over the fruit. Stand the dishes in a roasting pan containing a little hot water and cook at 180°C(350°F)/Gas 4 for 30 minutes, until the custard is set. Remove the dishes from the oven.

Increase the heat to 190°C(375°F)/Gas 5 while you make the meringue topping. Stiffly whisk the egg white, beat in half the remaining caster sugar and beat again until the mixture is smooth and glossy. Fold in the rest of the sugar, using a metal spoon, and spread the meringue over the custard tops, piling it to a peak in the centre. Return the dishes to the roasting pan and cook for 5 minutes to brown the meringue.

The custards can be served warm or cold, with sponge finger biscuits (see page 121).
*Serves 4*

## Apple Frost

A simple family pudding that's a good way to use up windfall apples, and spare egg whites.

*450 g (1 lb) cooking apples, peeled, cored and chopped*
*2 tablespoons lemon juice*
*50 g (2 oz) sugar*
*2 tablespoons water*
*1 teaspoon powdered gelatine*
*pinch nutmeg*
*150 ml (5 fl oz) natural yoghurt, chilled*
*2 egg whites, stiffly beaten*
*cloves to decorate*

Put the prepared apple in a pan with the lemon juice and half the sugar and cook over a moderate heat until the fruit is soft. Rub through a sieve or put in a blender. Put the water in a small bowl, sprinkle on the gelatine and stand in a larger bowl of hot water. Stir to dissolve the gelatine, allow to cool a little, then pour into the apple pulp, beating to blend well. Beat in the remaining sugar, nutmeg and yoghurt and whisk until the mixture is light and frothy. Fold in the stiffly-beaten egg whites and spoon into 4 individual fruit bowls. Serve chilled.

To decorate, make a pattern of an apple core with radiating cloves on the top of each bowl.
*Serves 4*


## Tipsy Oranges

Sometimes the very simplicity of a dessert is welcome, particularly when the main dish is rich and filling, say a meat pudding or pie. But presentation then becomes even more important.

*4 large oranges*
*1 tablespoon orange liqueur*
*100 g (4 oz) black grapes, halved and seeded (reserve 4 halves to decorate)*
*300 ml (10 fl oz) natural yoghurt, chilled (or use 2 cartons of the commercial orange-flavoured variety)*
*15 g (¹/₂ oz) caster sugar*
*4 sprigs mint to decorate*

Cut a very thin slice from the base of each orange, just enough to make the fruit stand firm. Then cut the top from each orange, just under one-third of the way down. Using a grapefruit knife, scoop the fruit from the shells and 'lids' and remove any pips and tough fibres. Put the orange flesh in a bowl and stir in the liqueur and grapes. Cover the container and chill in the refrigerator or a cold place.

Drain the orange shells and put them in the freezer or freezing compartment of the refrigerator to frost.

When you are ready to serve the fruit, stir the chilled yoghurt into the orange mixture. Dip the rims of the orange shells in caster sugar and spoon in the fruit. Decorate each one with a reserved grape and a sprig of mint.

Wash the orange shells after serving and freeze them to use as containers for Orange Mousse (see next recipe).
*Serves 4*


## Orange Mousse

This recipe makes second-time-around use of orange shells as decorative containers.

*1 small can frozen concentrated orange juice, thawed*
*100 g (4 oz) caster sugar*
*3 eggs, separated*
*150 ml (5 fl oz) natural yoghurt, whipped*
*a few blanched almonds, toasted, to decorate*

Heat the orange juice and sugar in a bowl resting on a pan of hot water. Beat the egg yolks until they are thick and creamy and stir them into the orange mixture. Cook over just simmering water, stirring occasionally, until the mixture thickens. Allow to cool, then fold in the whipped yoghurt and stiffly-beaten egg whites.

Spoon the mousse into four orange shells and serve chilled, decorated with toasted almonds.
*Serves 4*

### Chestnut Chocolate Cream
Chestnuts and chocolate is one of my favourite combinations. This pudding tastes luxurious, but is made in a trice.

*225 g (8 oz) plain chocolate, broken into squares*
*175 g (6 oz) unsweetened chestnut purée*
*25 g (1 oz) butter, softened*
*25 g (1 oz) icing sugar, sifted*
*2 tablespoons brandy*
*1 teaspoon instant coffee powder*
*1 tablespoon water, hot*
*300 ml (10 fl oz) natural yoghurt, chilled and whipped*
*75 g (3 oz) blanched almonds, slivered and toasted, to decorate*

Melt the chocolate in a bowl over a pan of hot water. Put the chestnut purée into a bowl and beat in the melted chocolate, softened butter, icing sugar and brandy. Dissolve the coffee powder in the hot water and slowly add to the chestnut mixture, beating well. Fold in the whipped yoghurt and blend well.

Turn the mixture into a serving bowl and leave in the refrigerator or a cold place to chill and set. To serve, stick the slivered almonds, hedgehog-prickle fashion, all over the top. Serve with sponge finger biscuits (see page 121).
*Serves 6*

### Caramel Peaches
This dish is so easy to make, yet so delicious. It looks most impressive for a party, with the peaches piled high into a pyramid.

*4 large, ripe peaches*
*150 g (5 oz) yoghurt cheese (see page 5)*
*1 tablespoon orange or apricot liqueur*

*1 tablespoon caster sugar*
*200 g (7 oz) soft light brown sugar*
*25 g (1 oz) butter*
*2 tablespoons milk*
*25 g (1 oz) blanched almonds, toasted*

Dip the peaches in boiling water, then remove the skins. Halve the peaches and remove the stones. Put the yoghurt cheese into a small bowl and beat in the liqueur and caster sugar. Sandwich the peach halves together with a filling of the cheese and secure them with tooth-picks or wooden cocktail sticks.

To make the sauce, put the brown sugar, butter and milk in a small pan and stir until the sugar dissolves. Bring to the boil and simmer for 7 minutes. Beat until the mixture starts to thicken.

Put the peaches in a serving dish and pour over the sauce, which will harden as it cools. Scatter with the nuts.
*Serves 4*

## Baked Peaches

*4 peaches*
*40 g (1¹/₂ oz) mixed candied peel, chopped*
*25 g (1 oz) blanched almonds, chopped*
*25 g (1 oz) soft dark brown sugar*
*2 tablespoons sweet sherry*
*100 g (4 oz) yoghurt cheese (see page 5)*
*1 tablespoon blanched almonds, toasted*

Dip the peaches in boiling water. Remove the skins, halve and stone the fruit and place the peach halves, cut sides up, in a shallow baking dish. Mix together two-thirds of the chopped peel, the chopped almonds and sugar and spoon the mixture into the peaches. Pour on the sherry and bake at 180°C(350°F)/Gas 4 for 15 minutes.

Stir the remaining chopped peel into the yoghurt cheese. Spoon over the peach halves and sprinkle with the toasted almonds. Serve hot or cold.
*Serves 4*

## Pineapple Fritters

Yoghurt cheese topping is good with all kinds of fruit fritters. Scatter chocolate drops on top of banana fritters, and raisins on fried apple rings.

*100 g (4 oz) flour*
*pinch salt*
*1 tablespoon vegetable oil*
*1 egg*
*150 ml (¹/₄ pint) milk*

*oil for frying*
*4 pineapple rings, drained (reserve syrup)*
*1 tablespoon pineapple syrup*
*1 tablespoon chopped canned pineapple (optional)*
*50 g (2 oz) yoghurt cheese (see page 5)*
*caster sugar to serve*

To make the fritter batter, sift the flour and salt into a bowl, make a well in the centre and add the oil, egg and milk. Beat well to form a smooth batter. Heat the oil in a deep pan. Pat the pineapple rings dry on kitchen paper and, using tongs or a fork, dip them in the batter. Fry the rings in hot oil for a few minutes until the coating batter is crisp and golden. Arrange the rings on a heated serving dish and keep warm.

Beat the pineapple syrup and chopped pineapple (if any is available) into the yoghurt cheese. Spoon the cheese into the centre of each pineapple ring and serve dredged with caster sugar.
*Serves 4*

### Chocolate Cheese Pancakes
The crunchiness of chocolate drops is an interesting discovery in this creamy cheese filling.

*100 g (4 oz) flour*
*pinch salt*
*1 egg*
*300 ml (¹/₂ pint) milk*
*1 tablespoon cooking oil*
*extra oil for frying*

For filling
*225 g (8 oz) yoghurt cheese (see page 5)*
*75 g (3 oz) seedless raisins*
*50 g (2 oz) chocolate drops*
*grated zest and juice of 1 lemon*
*caster sugar to decorate*
*lemon wedges to serve (optional)*

To make the pancakes, sift the flour and salt into a bowl, beat in the egg and half the milk. Beat well, then pour in the remainder of the milk and the cooking oil. Beat well until the mixture is smooth. Leave the batter to rest for 30 minutes before cooking the pancakes.

Heat a little oil in a heavy-based omelette or frying pan and, when a faint haze begins to rise, pour off the oil, leaving just enough to grease the base of the pan. Pour in a little batter and tilt the pan so that the batter extends to the edges. Cook the pancake over a moderate-to-high heat until the top is set and the underside golden brown. Flip the pancake over with a spatula, or toss by holding the pan firmly and quickly flicking your wrist. Cook until the other side of the pancake browns, then slide it on to a warm dish or plate. If you are serving the pancakes straightaway, keep the cooked ones hot while you cook the others. If not, allow the pancakes to cool, then wrap them in foil and store in the refrigerator or freeze them.

To make the filling, beat the yoghurt cheese and stir in the raisins, chocolate drops and lemon zest and juice. Beat well to blend.

Divide the filling between the hot pancakes, roll up and dredge with caster sugar. Serve, if liked, with lemon wedges.

If you have stored the pancakes, reheat them in foil or a covered dish in the oven and then fill and serve them as described.

*Makes about 8 pancakes*


## Baked Yoghurt Custards
A traditional favourite in a slightly new form.

*4 egg yolks*
*50 g (2 oz) sugar*
*300 ml (10 fl oz) natural yoghurt*
*ground nutmeg*

Beat together the egg yolks and sugar until creamy, then beat in the yoghurt until well blended. Pour into four individual soufflé dishes and sprinkle each with ground nutmeg. Stand them in a roasting pan with hot water to come halfway up the sides of the dishes. Bake at 180°C(350°F)/Gas 4 for 30 minutes until the custards are set. Allow the custards to cool, then chill them in the refrigerator. Serve with fresh or stewed fruit.

*Serves 4*


## Burnt Yoghurt Cream
Burnt cream, sometimes called Crème Brulée, bayleaves and nutmeg – a very nineteenth-century combination.

*300 ml (¹/₂ pint) double cream*
*300 ml (10 fl oz) natural yoghurt*
*2 bayleaves*
*freshly-grated nutmeg*
*4 egg yolks*
*75 g (3 oz) caster sugar*
*extra bayleaves to decorate*

In a double boiler or a bowl over a pan of hot water, slowly heat the double cream and yoghurt with the bayleaves and a few gratings of nutmeg. When the cream is just below boiling point, remove it from the heat. Beat the egg yolks with

137

one-third of the caster sugar and pour on to the cream, stirring all the time. Return to a low heat and cook gently until the custard thickens. Strain the custard into six small cocotte dishes. Sprinkle the tops with the remaining sugar and cook under a hot grill until it caramellizes. Decorate each dish with a bayleaf.
*Serves 6*

## Bread and Butter Pudding
Everyone seems to have a different recipe for bread and butter pudding, according, in most cases it seems, to how nanny or mother made it in nursery days. In our family now, we like the custard made with yoghurt.

*4 thin slices of bread, buttered*
*50 g (2 oz) sultanas*
*50 g (2 oz) currants*
*50 g (2 oz) caster sugar*
*150 ml (¼ pint) milk*
*2 eggs*
*300 ml (5 fl oz) natural yoghurt*
*¼ teaspoon vanilla essence*
*grated nutmeg*
*extra caster sugar to decorate*

Cut the crusts from the bread and cut the slices into triangles. Butter a 1-litre (2-pint) ovenproof dish and arrange the bread in layers with the dried fruit and half the sugar. Put the milk and remaining sugar in a small pan and heat until the sugar has dissolved – an occasional stir will help. Beat the eggs, yoghurt and vanilla essence together and stir into the milk. Strain this mixture on to the bread and fruit and leave to stand for 30 minutes. Sprinkle nutmeg on top and bake at 180°C(350°F)/Gas 4, for 45 minutes, until the custard is set and golden brown. Sprinkle with more caster sugar to serve.
*Serves 4*

## Dairy Cheese Cake
Rich with butter, yoghurt cheese and eggs, this flan would be a fitting pudding to serve at the end of a farmhouse-type meal.

*175 g (6 oz) flour*
*¼ teaspoon salt*
*75 g (3 oz) butter*
*25 g (1 oz) caster sugar*
*1 egg yolk*
*1 tablespoon water*

For filling
*225 g (8 oz) yoghurt cheese (see page 5)*

*2 eggs, separated*
*50 g (2 oz) sugar*
*grated zest and juice of ¹/₂ lemon*
*25 g (1 oz) butter, softened*
*25 g (1 oz) sultanas*
*25 g (1 oz) currants*

For topping
*1 egg, beaten*
*15 g (¹/₂ oz) sugar*
*15 g (¹/₂ oz) flour*
*15 g (¹/₂ oz) butter, melted*

Grease a 20-cm (8-in) flan ring and baking sheet or a flan case.

To make the pastry, sift the flour and salt into a bowl, rub in the butter with the fingertips until the mixture resembles fine breadcrumbs, and stir in the sugar. Beat together the egg yolk and water and stir into the mixture. Mix to a firm dough and knead lightly on a floured surface. Wrap the dough in foil and chill in the refrigerator or a cold place for 30 minutes. Roll out thinly on a floured board and use to line the flan ring or flan case. Trim the edges and prick the pastry base.

To make the filling, beat together the yoghurt cheese, beaten egg yolks, sugar, lemon rind and juice and softened butter, and stir in the dried fruit. Fold in the stiffly-beaten egg whites and pour the filling into the pastry case.

To make the topping, mix together the egg, sugar, flour and melted butter and spread over the filling.

Bake at 180°C(350°F)/Gas 4 for 40 minutes, until the top is golden brown. Serve cold.
*Serves 6*


## Butterscotch Cream Flan
For a lighter flan base, you can use a cooked sponge flan ring, home-made or bought, instead of the pastry

*25 g (1 oz) butter*
*1 dessertspoon golden syrup*
*25 g (1 oz) soft dark brown sugar*
*450 ml (³/₄ pint) milk*
*40 g (1¹/₂ oz) cornflour*
*150 ml (5 fl oz) natural yoghurt*
*100 g (4 oz) walnuts, halved*
*1 20-cm (8-in) pastry case, baked blind (see page 58)*

Put the butter, syrup and sugar into a pan and stir over a gentle heat until the sugar dissolves. Remove from the heat, allow the mixture to cool slightly, then add all but two tablespoons of the milk. Return the pan to the heat and stir well. Allow the mixture to heat but not boil. Put the cornflour into a small bowl and pour on the reserved milk, mixing to a smooth paste. Pour a little of the hot milk into the bowl, stir, and pour it into the pan. Cook over a low heat, stirring until the mixture thickens. Remove the pan from the heat, allow to cool a little and stir in the yoghurt.

Reserve five walnuts to decorate. Roughly chop the remainder and scatter them in the base of the pastry or sponge case. Pour on the butterscotch cream and leave to cool. When the filling has set, decorate with the reserved walnuts.
*Serves 6–8*

## Sweet Cheese Tart

Lemon and honey perfectly complement the yoghurt cheese in this quick-to-make cold dessert.

*225 g (8 oz) digestive biscuits*
*75 g (3 oz) butter*
*3 tablespoons clear honey*
*15 g (¹/₂ oz) powdered gelatine*
*4 tablespoons water*
*225 g (8 oz) yoghurt cheese (see page 5)*
*150 ml (5 fl oz) natural yoghurt*
*¹/₂ teaspoon vanilla essence*
*grated zest and juice of ¹/₂ lemon*
*75 g (3 oz) dates, stoned and chopped*
*thin lemon slices to decorate*

Put the biscuits in a polythene bag and crush them with a rolling pin, or crumb them in a blender. Put the butter and one tablespoon honey in a small pan over a low heat to melt. Stir in the biscuit crumbs and press into the base of a 20-cm (8-in) flan case. Leave to cool while making the filling.

Sprinkle the gelatine on the water in a small bowl, stand it in hot water and stir to dissolve. Beat the yoghurt cheese with the yoghurt until smooth, then stir in the remaining honey, vanilla essence, lemon zest and juice and the chopped dates. Beat well, then gradually pour on the gelatine. Blend thoroughly, then pour the filling into the cooled crumb base. Leave in the refrigerator or a cold place to set.

Decorate with fans or butterfly shapes arranged with quartered lemon slices.
*Serves 6*

## Pear Flan

Ginger in the crumb base and a gingered fruit filling make a spicy combination.

*175 g (6 oz) flour*
*1 tablespoon ground ginger*

*75 g (3 oz) butter*
*25 g (1 oz) caster sugar*
*1 egg yolk*
*1 tablespoon water*

For filling
*3 large dessert pears, peeled, cored and halved (or use canned pear halves)*
*2 tablespoons water*
*300 ml (10 fl oz) natural yoghurt*
*2 eggs, beaten*
*2 pieces stem ginger, finely chopped*
*1 tablespoon ginger syrup*
*1 tablespoon caster sugar*
*pinch ground ginger to decorate*

Grease a 20-cm (8-in) flan ring.

To make the pastry, sift the flour and ground ginger together in a bowl, rub in the butter until the mixture resembles fine breadcrumbs, then stir in the sugar. Beat the egg yolk and water and stir into the mixture. Mix to a firm dough, knead on a lightly-floured surface and wrap in foil. Chill the dough in the refrigerator or a cool place for at least 30 minutes. Roll the dough out on a lightly-floured board and use to line the flan ring. Line the pastry base with greased greaseproof paper, fill with baking beans and bake 'blind' at 200°C(400°F)/Gas 6 for 15 minutes. Remove the foil and beans and bake for a further 7–8 minutes to dry the pastry.

To make the filling, put the fresh pears in a pan with the water, cover and gently poach them for 5 minutes. Drain them thoroughly. If using canned pears, drain them well.

Beat together the yoghurt and eggs and stir in the chopped ginger, syrup and caster sugar. Spoon half the filling into the pastry case and bake at 190°C(375°F)/Gas 5 for 20 minutes. Arrange the pear halves cut side down in a wheel pattern on top, spoon the remaining yoghurt mixture over and return to the oven for a further 10–12 minutes, until the custard is set. Sprinkle the top with a pinch of ground ginger. Serve the flan hot or cold.
*Serves 6*


**Fruit Tarts**
The creamy yoghurt topping is a perfect contrast to the dried fruit filling, acting like a delicate sauce.

*225 g (8 oz) flour*
*1/4 teaspoon salt*
*100 g (4 oz) butter*
*2–3 tablespoons water*

For filling
*2 large cooking apples, peeled, cored and grated*
*50 g (2 oz) dried apricots, soaked overnight in water*
*50 g (2 oz) seedless raisins*
*25 g (1 oz) mixed candied peel, chopped*
*25 g (1 oz) blanched almonds, toasted and slivered*
*50 g (2 oz) soft dark brown sugar*
*1/4 teaspoon mixed ground spice*
*grated zest and juice of 1 orange*

For topping
*300 ml (10 fl oz) natural yoghurt*
*2 egg yolks, beaten*
*50 g (2 oz) blanched almonds, flaked and toasted*

Grease 2 trays of patty tins.

To make the pastry, sift the flour and salt into a bowl and rub in the butter until the mixture resembles fine breadcrumbs, then stir in enough water to make stiff dough. Knead on a lightly-floured surface and roll the dough out thinly. Using a 9-cm (3½-in) pastry cutter, cut the dough into about twenty circles, re-rolling the trimmings. Line the patty tins with the dough.

To make the filling, put the grated apple in a bowl. Quarter the soaked apricots and add them to the apple with the rest of the filling ingredients. Stir well and spoon the mixture into the pastry. Level the tops with the back of a spoon. Bake at 200°C(400°F)/Gas 6 for 15 minutes and remove from the oven.

To make the topping, beat together the yoghurt and egg yolks and spoon over the tarts. Return to the oven for a further 8–10 minutes, to set the custard. Sprinkle with the toasted almonds.

*Makes about 20 tarts*

# *Index*

147